RESPONSE 1

Perhaps the best way we can avoid the pitfalls in our spiritual life is to open our spiritual eyes to perspectives we have not seen before. *Forecasting Temptation* speaks to this experience, which is so necessary for all of us. Dr. Butler speaks insightfully, in practical and real ways. Read this book and think it over deeply. There are no easy shortcuts in life, but this book will help guide you on your journey.

DAVID ZAILER, EXECUTIVE DIRECTOR, OPERATION INTEGRITY
AUTHOR, *WHEN LOST MEN COME HOME* AND *OUR JOURNEY HOME*

Forecasting Temptation looks mainly at the spiritual dynamics of temptation and key aspects of our relationship to it as believers. Dr. Butler doesn't seem to leave any rock unturned in anticipating the effects of temptation on our journeys and gives helpful, nearly-comprehensive strategies from a faith perspective that can help a person begin to deal with temptation in proactive, healthy ways towards a more well-rounded, God-honoring recovery and lifestyle.

JAYSON GRAVES, M.MFT., FOUNDER AND CLINICAL DIRECTOR
HEALING FOR THE SOUL COUNSELING

If you are breathing, you are dealing with temptation in your life. Randy's book, *Forecasting Temptation*, presents a practical, sensible, and applicable way to hand Satan a few defeats and for you to begin finding victory in your walk with the Lord. Wouldn't that be nice for a change? I know my walk could certainly use some once in a while!

TODD W. PYNCH, EXECUTIVE DIRECTOR
CRISIS CHAPLAINCY SERVICES; CHAPLAIN AT GROUND ZERO

Temptations touch each and every one of us. As a police officer, I see daily how acting on our temptations can ruin lives. Randy Butler's book, *Forecasting Temptation*, is like a roadmap to assist us on our journey through this life in making the right choices.

SERGEANT JEFF GOODMAN, KEIZER POLICE DEPARTMENT, OR

Forecasting Temptation

Stay close to God!
Phil. 4:13

FORECASTING Temptation

How to Anticipate the Storms
Before They Strike

RANDY R. BUTLER

Randy R. Butler

Deep River
BOOKS

Forecasting Temptation

Published by
Deep River Books
Sisters, Oregon
http://www.deepriverbooks.com

ISBN- 13: 9781937756123
ISBN- 10: 1937756122

Library of Congress: 2012939647

Printed in the USA

Cover design by Jeff Miller millerjef20@hotmail.com

Dedication

This book is dedicated to the men and women of law enforcement. These are the special people (family) I have been assigned to at the Keizer Police Department.

H. Marc Adams, Chief of Police
Jeffrey K. Kuhns, Captain
Alan McCowan, Lieutenant, Patrol Division
John Troncoso, Lieutenant, Criminal Investigation Division
Greg Barber, Patrol Sergeant
Andrew Copeland, Patrol Sergeant
Jeffrey Goodman, Patrol Sergeant
David LeDay, Traffic Unit Sergeant
Bob Trump, Sergeant
Trevor Wenning, Patrol Sergeant
Rita Powers, Police Services Supervisor
Wanda Blaylock, Administrative Assistant
Carrie Anderson, Police Officer
Arsen Avetisyan, Police Officer
David Babcock, Police Officer
Rodney Bamford, Police Officer
Scott Bigler, Police Officer
Dan Carroll, Police Officer
Kevin DeMarco, Police Officer
Vaughn Edsall, Detective
Jeremie Fletcher, Police Officer
Lynn Halladey, Community Services Officer
Ben Howden, Detective
Eric Jefferson, Traffic Unit Officer
Jeff Johnson, Police Officer
Dan Kelley, Traffic Unit Officer
Scott Keniston, K-9 Officer

Tim Lathrop, Detective
Prajedes Martinez, Police Support Specialist
Chris Nelson, Police Officer
BJ Olafson, Police Officer
Laurie Phillips, Investigative Support Specialist
Jay Prall, School Resource Officer
Ronna Price, Police Support Specialist
Stephen Richardson, K-9 Officer
Tyler Wampler, Police Officer
Jeremy Worledge, Police Officer
David Zavala, Police Officer
Richard Cummings, Reserve Police Officer

And, in loving memory of Sheila ("Shayla") Lisbeth Goodman
December 18, 1991 – August 28, 2010

Preface

I wrote this book because, having been raised in the church, I have watched as certain subjects were ignored—from my earliest memories of church life to the present day. Temptation is one of those ignored subjects. I suppose it is because it is so closely connected to sin.

However, this book separates temptation from sin. I separate it in a way that I am certain may upset some, but may greatly relieve others. My intent is neither to upset nor to relieve. My intent is to have an honest conversation about a subject that is truly the 800-pound gorilla in the room.

I trust the content of this book will help you do a better job in forecasting temptation, and thereby have a stronger relationship with God and the people you care about the most in your life.

Thanks for having courage to confront temptation!

TABLE OF CONTENTS

Foreword

I have known Randy for close to twenty years, and I have the privilege of being a member of the church where he is currently pastoring. My ministry is serving the community as a police officer. I began my law enforcement career just about as green as they come. I still remember my first day on the job; I could not stop smiling. My field training officer sat across the briefing room table and told me to knock it off in his gruff, seasoned-cop voice. It took me about two seconds to realize I might be in over my head. Thanks to God's grace, great field training officers, and great supervisors, I am still serving as an officer today.

I became a law enforcement officer to make a difference in the lives of the people in my community. I weigh heavily on values such as honor, integrity, trust, honesty, and being fair. As I put on my dark blue uniform of righteousness, gold badge of faith, black, polished boots that are fitted with the readiness of the gospel, and, finally, my duty belt of truth, I pray that this will not be my last shift. I pray that the next call I respond to will not be the final one.

I remember stopping a vehicle in the late hours of the night for a minor lighting violation in a residential neighborhood. I walked up to the window thinking I might have pulled over a local criminal or possibly an intoxicated driver. When I contacted the driver, I realized I did not stop either one of those. I found myself talking with a younger, fairly attractive female. The driver had all the right paperwork and had a valid license, so I gave her a verbal warning and sent her on her way. I walked back to my vehicle and waited in the area to observe another traffic violation when, to my surprise, the same vehicle pulled up behind me and the female driver got out. I initially thought she was going to be mad at me for pulling her over, but it was quite the opposite. I exited my vehicle and I found myself in the exact ethical, moral place I never want to be placed in. This young, attractive female asked me if I was married. Without hesitation I told her I was married, and the conversation was over. How differently that scenario could have played out if I was not prepared. I had previously rehearsed in my mind what I would do in that type of situation, so I was mentally prepared. I did not know it at the time but I was forecasting temptation.

Every month I receive an ethics bulletin that summarizes police officers, firefighters, and corrections officers that have made poor decisions and are now losing their certifications. These professionals are referred to as Officer A, Officer B, and so on, to keep their anonymity. I have seen the careers of some great people fall by the wayside because they fell into temptation. The temptation for police officers, firefighters, and corrections officers are fairly predictable: alcohol, money, and sex. So the question is, how can we as a professional community stop falling into temptations? *Forecasting Temptation* gives simple, real-life answers to fighting temptation. I often sit around a briefing table and talk with my team about not being the next Officer A in an ethics bulletin. Having the right mindset and being able to forecast temptation is vital for the battles I face.

Heraclitus wrote, "Out of every hundred men, ten should not be there, eighty are just targets, nine are the real fighters, and we are lucky to have them, for they make the battle. Ah, but the one, one is a warrior, and he will bring the others back." This was the first quote I thought of after I read this book. Heraclitus wrote this in reference to battle and overcoming the enemy, but how perfect it is when talking about overcoming temptation. In this world we live in, temptation is our enemy and we need to become the warrior. We see people all around us falling victim to temptation. There are a few that fight it valiantly, but we want—no, we need to be—the one that stands out as the warrior. Temptation can spring upon us at any moment and, if we are not prepared, if we do not have the right mindset, then we will succumb to evil and temptation, and give the devil a foothold in our lives. This book gives us every tool we need to be the warrior that every battle needs.

If you are familiar with law enforcement, the next two words might resonate with you: *reasonable suspicion*. Police officers live by those two words. For those of you not familiar with reasonable suspicion, I will give you a brief definition. Reasonable suspicion in reference to law enforcement is defined this way: Given the totality of the circumstances, it is more likely than not that a crime is about to be committed or was just committed. Reasonable suspicion gives law enforcement officers the lawful right to stop and detain someone. Temptation is just like reasonable suspicion, so let's change the definition just a little: Given the totality of the circumstances, it is more likely than not that a sin is about to be committed. Why are we so good at being able to sniff out crimes, but blind or unresponsive to the sins we are tempted with? I just wish I was as good at recognizing sin as I am at finding criminals.

Over a year ago, I was working night shift, and I observed a vehicle leaving a high-crime apartment complex around two in the morning. The vehicle was going the opposite direction than I, so I had to turn around. By the time I turned around, the driver had accelerated quickly away from me and made two turns. I was able to locate the vehicle, but the driver bailed and the vehicle was no longer occupied. I called for a couple of other units to start heading my way and then I began searching the area for my driver. Approximately a minute later, I observed a male coming out of a mobile home park just to the north of the vacant vehicle. The male was breathing heavy, sweating, and was not from the area. I quickly asked him his name and, sure enough, he had been stopped a few months ago in the same vehicle, according to our data base. I am not a detective, but I thought that might be a clue.

How often is sin that obvious? All the signs and symptoms are there, but for some reason we miss them. Temptation can be obvious and predictable; we just need to know how to forecast. This book helps teach the reader how to develop reasonable suspicion, so they can lawfully stop temptation before the sin is committed. I continued to riddle my exhausted new friend with a few more questions and, sure enough, he confessed to being the driver, fleeing, and having drugs in the vehicle.

Forecasting Temptation does not pass judgment nor does it excuse sinful behavior. Randy spells out how temptation can attack and the methods the devil uses to tempt people, and he gives real-life ways to defeat temptation. I pray as you read and as you are lead by the power of the Holy Spirit, you will be able to forecast temptation and then defeat it. I know we will be conquerors in Christ together, as temptation loses its foothold in our lives. Remember, "God did not give us a spirit of timidity, but a spirit of power, of love and of self-discipline" (2 Tim 1:7 NIV).

The information inside this book will change my life forever. I only pray that your heart and mind are open to the Spirit's leading, as you begin this life-changing adventure.

—Andrew Copeland
Police Sergeant
Previous SWAT Member;
Instructor: defensive tactics, reality-based training,
firearms, use of force;
2004 Officer of the Year;
2011 Gold Medalist:Toughest Competitor Alive,
Western States Police and Fire Games;
2012 Medal of Valor Recipient

Introduction

As a native Oregonian, my love of storms doesn't get much excitement to satisfy it. My family has enjoyed living in the Salem/Keizer area, in the heart of the Willamette Valley, since 1986. Our summers are pleasant, and the winters are mild. I live sixty miles from the ocean with a mountain range between us, nestled between the Coastal Range and the Cascade Mountain Range. Winter in the Willamette Valley means we might get one or two snow events—or none, some years. Usually, the forecast is more exciting than the storm itself. The TV meteorologists track the fronts and high and low pressure areas with their animated maps to plot the various possible outcomes. (No comment on how often their predictions are correct! We continue to pay attention to them, so we sort of trust them.) Whenever the first hint of a possible—maybe, sort of, but probably not going to happen—snow forecast appears, my dad calls me just to get my hopes up. We've been doing this since I was a little boy.

He called this past winter when the forecast was for the possibility—maybe, sort of, but probably not going to happen—of snow in the Willamette Valley. Where I live, we're such pansies that school gets canceled whenever snow is even forecasted.

My greatest year of snow was when I lived in Spokane, Washington, in 1984–1985. We had weeks of snow and weeks of freezing weather. It was awful—actually being in the storm was nothing like the fun of waiting for it. The romance of the idea of the storm seems much more appealing than the storm itself. And that's the way it is with temptation.

There are many temptations that look really good as we see the situations on our life map coming together, much like the fronts on a weather map. But in reality they are very dangerous. In fact, if the temptation you're considering doesn't look really good, there are others out there that will look better if you look a little harder! That is the nature of temptation. It's like a drug, and we go for more, bigger, better each and every time. We are rarely satisfied. It has been said that when asked what it would take to please man, the answer always comes back, "Just a little bit more." It begins as something very exciting and ends with a disaster. Not every time—but that's part of the lure. Disaster comes when we think we are in control.

I invite you to join me in a very honest conversation on the subject of forecasting temptation. We can quite accurately predict an upcoming temptation as we watch things come on to the radar of our lives. Just as we watch weather forecasts and take the necessary measures to protect ourselves from the potential danger, we can do the same thing with temptation—track it and stay out of harm's way.

—∾—

My goal for you is to discover your weaknesses, forecast the storms of your life, and discover ways to avoid the destruction that temptation often leaves behind. I have had many close calls with temptation. I have had victory over temptation, and too many times I have been damaged and hurt by temptation. So have you.

While you can read it on your own, this entire book is designed to be used as a discussion guide on the subject of temptation. It was written in a style meant to bring about a conversation. Each chapter is followed by Scriptures and lesson plans for study together. Use it in small groups, in Sunday school, for family devotions, in youth group, in church settings, or wherever you so choose. It is meant to lead people into a lot of meaningful and helpful conversations so we can get a better handle on temptation.

I use the word *temptation* throughout this book in such a way as to almost give it an identity, a life of its own. I did this because I believe it does take on a life of its own. I know there are times I use the word temptation when you might think Satan or one of his other names would be more appropriate. I did this so we would not underestimate the beast I call temptation.

Lastly, I did not write this book as an authority. I wrote this book because I am a victim. Like you, I have been victimized by temptation. I am tired of seeing what it has done to my life and to many others I love. Our world is a mess because temptation is winning the battle. It is imperative that we win the war. To this end, I hope this book helps you to better forecast temptation.

CHAPTER 1

We All Can Get Messed Up; There Are No Perfect Christians!

I became a Christian when I was seven years old. I have been on a quest for perfection for more than 45 years. Between the ages of 7 and 17, I was a frequent flyer at altar calls at my church. I was in constant search of perfection. The harder I tried, the more miserable I became. It was a very frustrating existence. I could not ever get victory or joy in my life because I was always striving for perfection.

As a teenager, I had a one-thousand-pound desk in my bedroom with a one-hundred-pound King James Bible that sat on the top. That Bible was light brown leather with a million pages in it. I figured that to be a perfect Christian, a big Bible was mandatory. I was wrong about that too! I spent hours reading my Bible, trying to learn all I could to perfect my Christianity. I was determined to be a perfect Christian.

It wasn't until more recently in my Christian journey that I understood it is about a covenant relationship with God far more than it is about using a bunch of rules as a measurement of how close I was getting to perfection. Further, I now understand better that even in relationships, you cannot have perfection. You can have a covenant, but not perfection, at least this side of heaven. I talk about this at length in my first book, *Reclaiming Heaven's Covenant: God's Blueprint to Restore All Relationships.*

I went to church every time the doors were open. In fact, I was at church at least thirty minutes ahead of schedule in order to greet people, help the pastor, and get the perfect seat in church so I could become a perfect Christian. So far, no such luck. I thought I was getting close once in a while, but I would mess up and be reminded that I had taken one step forward and two steps backward.

Every opportunity that arose in the life of the church, I volunteered for, because I figured that was part of being a perfect Christian. I did everything you can do in the church, including working in the nursery—and I hated working in the nursery. But if you are going to achieve perfection, you have to love that which you love the least in order to be perfect, don't you?

(Actually, I love children and I love babies, I just cannot stomach what happens south of the border. I gag every time I smell a diaper! My wife, on the other hand, has no sniffer and has worked in our church nursery since day one. What a gift!)

When I was in high school, our church built a new building. I did not have much money but I gave the vast majority of what I had saved for college back in the 1970s ($500) to the effort. You see, part of becoming a perfect Christian means you give away more money than you make, don't you?

I went to a Christian college, because the only real way to become perfect is to go to a Christian college, right?

I chose not to date, though if the truth be known there was nobody really interested in me until my third year in college. So, to fit the perfect Christian syndrome, I chose to be the Protestant version of a monk. I was going to be single my entire life and work 169 hours a week for God, because in order to be perfect you have to work one hour more than what is humanly possible, right?

Naturally I became a pastor, because to become a perfect Christian you have to be a pastor, which meant I really felt sorry for all other Christians who never had a chance at becoming perfect. I worked long hours to demonstrate my march toward perfection.

Every day, I tried to get one more person to come to church because a part of being a perfect Christian pastor is a growing church, right? I was happy only once in a great while, because the nature of perfection is never really being able to enjoy much of anything in life.

I also tried to make sure everybody always liked me, all the time, because that is certainly a part of being a perfect Christian. I have gone to enormous lengths in my life to please people because I thought that must be a part of being a perfect Christian too.

I could write volumes on the thousands of ways I worked to be a perfect Christian, but that would only show the many ways I am not a perfect Christian. The reality of life is that there are no perfect Christians. I know—I've been trying for more than 45 years! If I lived to be as old as Methuselah, I still could not reach perfection. It's true. All of us can get messed up. When it comes to perfection, evolution is a really bad myth. In Christianity, there is a myth stating that "the longer you are a Christian the better you become." What it implies is that perfection is attainable in this life. No, it is not. I have been trying to become perfect for more than forty-five years, and I am not even close to perfection. In fact, I stink. It's not that I am making excuses for sin. I am stating a reality about Christianity. I am not making a case for bad behavior. I am simply telling you there are no perfect Christians.

There is a tremendous beauty and freedom in embracing our humanity. Beauty is not in perfection. Beauty comes in imperfection. Like a piece of wood, the beauty is not in its sameness throughout but in its knots and imperfections. Our uniqueness comes when we are vulnerable and weak and needy and helpless and imperfect. The perception of perfection is very ugly. It smells of superiority and pride.

While I never am going to be perfect, I certainly do not want to become a slave to temptation either. I believe we can forecast temptation. In forecasting temptation, we can avoid some really bad storms in life. In forecasting temptation, we can avoid some very dangerous white-outs and driving conditions we ought not to be out in. And, like the weather, forecasting does not always mean we can avoid the storm. But it sure helps to know there is a storm brewing somewhere out there and that it is heading our way.

Temptation is a storm. All storms are vicious. That is the nature of a storm. If it were not vicious, it would not be called a storm. The problem with "perfection" is that people think they can outweather any storm in life. Worse, they live under the illusion that the storm cannot hurt them. The reality is that simply just is not true. Someone trying to be perfect will fight the winds of temptation. One trying to be wise will run from the whisper of temptation. The two are vastly different. There are enough problems in life; we do not need to be storm chasers.

Someone trying to be perfect will fight the winds of temptation. One trying to be wise will run from the whisper of temptation. The two are vastly different.

The first key to fighting temptation is to understand that all of us can get messed up; thus, we are in this thing together. It is time we take some medicine called *honesty* and quit trying to be something we are not. I have been a minister since 1980. I am tired of trying to be perfect. But I am not tired of trying to live in a relationship with Jesus Christ. In short, God is not after my perfection; if that were true, I would not need Him! God is after *me.* He loves me just the way I am. He is after a relationship, not perfection.

TEMPTATION – GENESIS 3:1–13

To prepare to forecast temptation, it is helpful to better recognize where temptation got its start. What took place in Genesis 3:1–13 is taking place today. Absolutely nothing has changed over these many years. Please carefully read this passage. They are not meant to be skimmed, but rather absorbed. I will make comments on this passage after you have read it. Genesis 3:1–13 reads:

> 1 Now the serpent was the most cunning of all the wild animals
> that the LORD God had made. He said to the woman, "Did God
> really say, 'You can't eat from any tree in the garden'?"
> 2 The woman said to the serpent, "We may eat the fruit from
> the trees in the garden. 3 But about the fruit of the tree in
> the middle of the garden, God said, 'You must not eat it or
> touch it, or you will die.'"
> 4 "No! You will not die," the serpent said to the woman. 5

> "In fact, God knows that when you eat it your eyes will be opened and you will be like God, knowing good and evil."
> 6 Then the woman saw that the tree was good for food and delightful to look at, and that it was desirable for obtaining wisdom. So she took some of its fruit and ate [it]; she also gave [some] to her husband, [who was] with her, and he ate
> [it]. 7 Then the eyes of both of them were opened, and they knew they were naked; so they sewed fig leaves together and made loincloths for themselves.
> 8 Then the man and his wife heard the sound of the LORD God walking in the garden at the time of the evening breeze, and they hid themselves from the LORD God among the trees of the garden.
> 9 So the LORD God called out to the man and said to him, "Where are you?"
> 10 And he said, "I heard You in the garden, and I was afraid because I was naked, so I hid."
> 11 Then He asked, "Who told you that you were naked? Did you eat from the tree that I had commanded you not to eat from?"
> 12 Then the man replied, "The woman You gave to be with me—she gave me [some fruit] from the tree, and I ate."
> 13 So the LORD God asked the woman, "What is this you have done?" And the woman said, "It was the serpent. He deceived me, and I ate."

Wow! What a revealing passage of Scripture on our humanity. We all really can get messed up. Adam and Eve were all messed up, and not much has changed since that day in the Garden of Eden. So much for perfection!

This passage is the foundation for temptation from that day to this day. It is worth taking a closer look at.

The first verse tells us a lot about our enemy and his beast called *temptation*. Our enemy is cunning and is an animal. He is not a purring kitty cat; he is a roaring lion. The first thing the enemy does is put a seed of doubt into our mind about the words of God. "Did God really say?" This is Satan's favorite line. He is always undermining the word of God. Of course God really said what He said. When Satan tells us for long enough that something isn't as it appears, we start to believe him. Remember, he is a liar and a thief!

Then we see in verse 4 how Satan directly contradicts the words of God. He said to Eve, "You will not die!" Satan is a liar. So far, the beast has not appeared, but it is about to make its first guest appearance onto the stage of planet earth. Verse 6 tells us, "The woman saw… delightful to look at…it was desirable." These are the three components of temptation. The enemy uses these to appeal to our senses, not our sensibility. Read them again. Memorize them. Don't ever forget this trilogy!

Verse 7 tells us about some of the consequences when we listen to temptation. Verse 8 tells us something else we do when we act out temptation: we hide from God. In our shame and regret, which is the result of temptation obeyed, God is still asking the question, "Where are you?" In spite of our shortcomings, God is still calling out for us. He is looking for people willing to follow His voice right to His Son Jesus Christ, who is the only one qualified to lead us away from temptation.

In verse 13, we learn the ultimate nature of temptation, which is deception. It says in verse 13: "He [the serpent] deceived me." Satan is a liar, and temptation is based on lies.

Together, we can have a conversation that will help all of us try to find a map back to the Garden of Eden. The purpose for going back is not to become perfect, but to have a relationship with God. If this conversation puts you on a road to a better relationship with God, then everybody wins except the devil. If it fails to complete that task, everybody loses except the devil. Don't let the devil win this one.

Scriptures on the Holy Spirit

1. Do not banish me from Your presence or take Your Holy Spirit from me (Psalm 51:11).

2. I baptize you with water for repentance, but the One who is coming after me is more powerful than I. I am not worthy to take off His sandals. He Himself will baptize you with the Holy Spirit and fire (Matthew 3:11).
3. The angel replied to her: "The Holy Spirit will come upon you, and the power of the Most High will overshadow you. Therefore the holy One to be born will be called the Son of God" (Luke 1:35).
4. If you then, who are evil, know how to give good gifts to your children, how much more will the heavenly Father give the Holy Spirit to those who ask Him? (Luke 11:13).
5. But the Counselor, the Holy Spirit—the Father will send Him in My name—will teach you all things and remind you of everything I have told you (John 14:26).
6. Then they were all filled with the Holy Spirit and began to speak in different languages, as the Spirit gave them ability for speech (Acts 2:4).
7. The circumcised believers who had come with Peter were astounded, because the gift of the Holy Spirit had been poured out on the Gentiles also (Acts 10:45).
8. Do you not know that your body is a sanctuary of the Holy Spirit who is in you, whom you have from God? You are not your own, for you were bought at a price; therefore glorify God in your body (1 Corinthians 6:19–20).
9. Now to Him who is able to do above and beyond all that we ask or think—according to the power that works in you—to Him be glory in the church and in Christ Jesus to all generations, forever and ever. Amen (Ephesians 3:20–21).
10. And don't grieve God's Holy Spirit, who sealed you for the day of redemption (Ephesians 4:30).

Lesson #1

1. Explore the two top temptations you struggle with most. Why are they so compelling?

2. Identify Scriptures you currently use to combat temptation.
3. Who are you accountable to with your struggles with temptation? What works? What is not working?
4. What is your greatest need concerning temptation as you begin this book?
5. It is good to ask questions about temptation. I would encourage you to use these as discussion starters, or if you are alone as reflection starters.

   Why do we do it?
   When do we do it?
   Where do we do it?
   What do we do?
   Who do we do it with?
6. Help…
   a. Involve the Holy Spirit in your struggle against temptation, very specifically asking Him to give you deliverance.
   b. Pray until you have victory over the temptations facing you right now.
   c. Pore over the Scriptures until one grabs you and you have an exit plan away from the temptation.
   d. Engage someone you trust with your battle against temptation so you can get more support in this battle.

CHAPTER 2

About Temptation

My wife volunteers her time at a store that sells inexpensive home furnishings. Once in a while she brings home a trinket for our house. Several days ago, she brought home this little wall hanging that says, "I feel a sin coming on." If that doesn't capture temptation, I don't know what does.

What exactly is temptation? Allow me to begin by saying that temptation is not sin. But it is very close to sin, and it can lead to sin. What Christmas Eve is to Christmas, temptation is to sin.

The entire human race deals with temptation. We are all the same at the foot of the cross. There is nobody other than Christ Himself qualified to rise higher than the level of the foot of the cross, since He is the only one without sin. My entire life I was taught a lot about sin and a little about temptation. But nobody ever taught me about forecasting temptation. I had never heard that phrase until I began writing this book. It is my hope that learning to forecast temptation will enable you to overcome it more regularly.

All sin comes through the gate of temptation. There is not another gate by which it enters. Temptation is nothing short of a necessary evil in our world—and it is not going away. For the one with an addiction, temptation is all-consuming. For the patient dying of cancer, temptation is less consuming; nonetheless, it is just as real, regardless of the circumstances.

Temptation, when yielded to, becomes sin.

Temptation that is not yielded to is not sin; it is defeated temptation. But it never goes very far away. It hides, waiting for the moment when a person is most vulnerable. Temptation is unfair, unkind, and underestimated.

Sin is disobedience to God's truths recorded in the Bible. Temptation is not disobedience to the Bible or anything else. Temptation is as natural as breathing air and drinking water. Temptation is a part of life. That is part of the problem; it is natural and common. We are so used to being tempted that we expect it at any moment. The problem is also that we, more often than not, expect to yield to it rather than resisting it.

Temptation is very deceiving in nature. Sometimes we are so friendly with it that we call it friend; yet temptation is more aggravating than hemorrhoids! Temptation starts out really good but ends up really bad, every single time. Temptation is never good. Walking away from temptation is always good. However, the nature of the temptation is never good.

Temptation looks desirable and attractive. It is strong, addicting, controlling, blinding, quick, potentially destructive, and always life-changing—always. It looks desirable in that it always invites us into something that we crave. Unfortunately, most of the things we crave in this life are not good for us. Take for instance Twinkies. I love that cream-filled pastry. I have eaten them since I was a child. In fact, I may have gone from nursing straight to Twinkies. But you and I both know how much good they actually do for me!

Temptation is attractive in that it is always dressed up and ready for you to take it out for a night on the town. Temptation is always ready to go whenever you are ready to go. Temptation is never late, rarely early, yet always on time. Temptation is strong in that it has the ability to overpower the strongest of Christians. There is not a single Christian on earth who has the power to say no to temptation every single time over a lifetime. That is why I say we all can get messed up, and there is no such thing as a perfect Christian.

Temptation is addicting. I don't know about you, but I have my favorite ones. Because I define them as favorite, they are an addiction for me. They are for you too, if you are honest. I am not a defeatist, rather a realist. I at least have the guts to say it.

Temptation is very controlling—controlling in the sense that it is almost as if I'm sometimes in a trance when dealing with certain temptations. Temptation is blinding in that it catches us off guard. In fact, if it did not catch us off guard, there would be no need for a book like this one. But because it does catch us off guard—like the waves at the beach—we need help.

I had a friend who was at the Oregon Coast looking for his brother who reportedly had been swept away by a wave at the beach. As he looked for his brother near the same location, he too was swept away and his life was snuffed out. This illustrates the blinding power temptation has over the strongest of individuals.

Temptation is quick. Before we realize what has happened to us, the crime has been committed; the deed has been done. It is as though time stands still, and while we are frozen in time, we do the stupidest things imaginable. Welcome to the world of temptation.

Temptation is potentially destructive. If it isn't destructive the first time you indulge, it certainly will be destructive over time. Give temptation enough opportunity and it will ruin the strongest of Christians. Shall we start naming the preachers, leaders, teachers, friends, and family members we know who have been swallowed up by temptation? I never look for temptation; it always finds me.

Temptation is always life-changing. Life is never the same after facing temptation. You either face temptation and win, which changes your perspective and exposes your need to be vigilant at all times; or you face temptation and lose, which alters the course of your life. There is no middle ground with temptation. Temptation has a slogan: "All or Nothing."

The longer you're a Christian, the stronger the temptations become. I have found this to be true in my life. I thought it should be the other way around, but it is not. I remember an elderly lady in our church. She is now in heaven. I distinctly remember her saying, "I wish that old Devil would leave me alone, but he just keeps tempting me, even when I'm an old lady!" She was the wife of a pastor for more than 50 years and probably never missed a day of church in her life—one of the godliest ladies I have ever known. If she couldn't lick temptation, what makes me think I can make it go away?

I still have some residual thinking patterns about trying to be a perfect Christian; yet the strength of the temptations I face remind me quite regularly that I can get all messed up. You see, I do not believe we are sort of perfect, or mostly perfect, or partly perfect, or perfect sometimes. The word *perfect* conveys absolute perfection, all of the time. I am willing to admit I have a chink in my armor; therefore, by definition I am messed up.

My only consolation (and we do it all the time as Christians) is to compare myself to others in the ways I strive for that elusive mark of perfection. I compare my mess to that of another, and sometimes think I am closer to perfect than the other person because he seems to be worse off than I am. That does not mean I am not messed up. It means in addition to being messed up, I am judgmental. Wow, I believe it's already time for another Twinkie!

I have discovered that temptation thrives in some unlikely places. Temptation seems to take root in fatigue, frustration, fighting, fretting, forgetting God, failure to forgive, and doubt.

Temptation finds root in fatigue, in that when I am tired, my senses are dulled. When my senses are dulled, I will do things I would never do otherwise. It's like being a little bit drunk; you know what you're doing, you just don't care enough to stop doing it. Have another beer.

Temptation incubates in the sea of frustration. When I am frustrated, I almost go looking for temptation. It never takes long to find, and for a short while—in my moment of frustration—I am temporarily satisfied by giving in to the temptation.

I find temptation takes root in fighting. In fact, temptation loves arguments because it becomes the cheerleader for both sides, cheering for both sides to keep on fighting. The fight always leads to something worse, and we have temptation to thank for the mess we find ourselves in.

Then there is the attitude of fretting. We fret when our view of God is smaller than our problems and there seems to be no way to deal with them. If the problems seem larger than God, we are ripe for temptation. We feel like we can figure out ways on our own to solve the problems.

We fret and stew and get all bent out of shape because in our fretting, we have lost sight of just how big God is.

Sadly, temptation grows in another ugly marsh called *forgetting God*. For being so important to Christians, He sure gets left behind and left out of a lot of things. This adds up to a failure to remember God. When we do this, temptation begins to yell for joy from the mountaintops. Forgetting God usually comes when we stop reading our Bible, going to church, praying—you get the idea. When we cut ourselves off from ways He can speak to us, it's easy to forget Him.

Temptation loves it when we don't want to forgive someone. That is the perfect fertilizer for temptation to grow and sprout wings in our life. And let's not forget hardcore failure. When we fail, we often self-destruct. Failure quickly searches out temptation because once you've failed, you might as well go big!

Finally, temptation's richest potting soil is doubt. It opens the way to make temptation definitely look better. Anybody who doubts might as well go to bed with temptation because at this point it's game over—game, set and match.

Something that must not be overlooked is the fact that temptation is very common. It's not special at all. In fact, it is as common as a penny. Yet it is more costly than a $100 bill. Your temptation is no more special than my temptation. We sometimes think we are facing something nobody else is facing. That is part of the nature of temptation; it is very deceptive.

I also find that temptation is not talked about much in the church. I suppose the reason few want to discuss it is because the next conversation might lead to topics like sin and addictions—and things get really messy in a hurry. We sure wouldn't want that in church now, would we? I mean, God forbid that we should talk about something that will actually help someone.

Talking about temptation in church becomes very personal and far too self-revealing. So let's talk about stuff that is someone else's problem, or let's talk about world problems, but let's stay far away from personal stuff like temptation.

Facing temptation takes a lot of preparedness. You can be better prepared by being a better forecaster of temptation in your life.

Repeated temptation that ends in failure causes a weird thought process. It kind of goes like this: Why try? The problem isn't the repeated temptation; it's the failure to forecast the temptation, and then it becomes too late to have success.

I must admit that I hate temptation because I actually know the difference between right and wrong. I'm over fifty years old and have been in the church my entire life. I pastor a fairly large church. I have read the Bible many times over. It's not like I don't know what is right and what is wrong.

This is why we need to have a conversation about temptation. Not one of us is ever free from it, no matter how long we've been a Christian. That leads me to an obvious point: Temptation seems to snag us and trip us up more than what it should. So I thought I'd come up with ways to forecast temptation, in order to do a better job of resisting it. I will never become a perfect Christian, but I can do a better job.

I want to make sure of something I believe is obvious, but it still needs to be said. Temptation is a part of life, and we have a choice to make about it. Temptation is not the work of another. I am its owner. I am responsible for my reaction to temptation. It knows me by name and I know it by name. And what I do with it is my choice.

Temptation is not the work of another. I am its owner. I am responsible for my reaction to temptation.

Something ought to be said about our past, too. We all have a story to tell. My past, my story, leads me to a set of temptations that will be a part of my life no matter the path I choose to walk. In other words, let's stop blaming our past for all the temptations before us today. Temptation does not live in the past or the future; it lives in the present, in order to ruin our future and wipe out our past. It is an evil enemy.

Ultimately, temptation cannot be avoided. If I joined a monastery, I'd find temptation somewhere on the property. If I attended a seminary, I'd find temptation there, too—especially there. If I live among the poor in Haiti, I'll find more temptation there than most anywhere else in the world. Wherever I go, temptation goes with me. It's the nature of the beast. You simply can't avoid it. But when you can forecast temptation, you'll be better equipped to deal with it.

Scriptures on the Blood

1. The blood on the houses where you are staying will be a distinguishing mark for you; when I see the blood, I will pass over you. No plague will be among you to destroy you when I strike the land of Egypt (Exodus 12:13).
2. Moses took the blood, sprinkled it on the people, and said, "This is the blood of the covenant that the Lord has made with you concerning all these words" (Exodus 24:8).
3. For this is My blood that establishes the covenant; it is shed for many for the forgiveness of sins (Matthew 26:28).
4. God presented Him as a propitiation through faith in His blood, to demonstrate His righteousness, because in His restraint God passed over the sins previously committed (Romans 3:25).
5. Much more then, since we have now been declared righteous by His blood, we will be saved through Him from wrath (Romans 5:9).
6. In the same way He also took the cup, after supper, and said, "This cup is the new covenant in My blood. Do this, as often as you drink it, in remembrance of Me" (1 Corinthians 11:25).
7. In Him we have redemption through His blood, the forgiveness of our trespasses, according to the riches of His grace that He lavished on us with all wisdom and understanding (Ephesians 1:7–8).
8. But if we walk in the light as He Himself is in the light, we have fellowship with one another, and the blood of Jesus His Son cleanses us from all sin. If we say, "We have no sin," we are deceiving ourselves, and the truth is not in us. If we confess our sins, He is faithful and righteous to forgive us our sins and to cleanse us from all unrighteousness (1 John 1:7–9).

9. And from Jesus Christ, the faithful witness, the firstborn from the dead and the ruler of the kings of the earth. To Him who loves us and has set us free from our sins by His blood, and made us a kingdom, priests, to His God and Father—to Him be the glory and the dominion forever and ever. Amen (Revelation 1:5–6).
10. I said to him, "Sir, you know." Then he told me: "These are the ones coming out of the great tribulation. They washed their robes and made them white in the blood of the Lamb" (Revelation 7:14).

LESSON #2

1. Genesis 3:1–13. Focus on the deception in this passage.
2. Genesis 39:1–23. Focus on what Joseph did to get away from the temptation. (Hint: He ran.)
3. Job1:1–22. Focus on how Job took care of business.
4. Matthew 4:1–11. Focus on how Jesus used Scripture to combat the enemy.
5. 1 John 2:1–6. Focus on the part that takes us beyond just belief.
6. Help…
   a. Ask the Holy Spirit to help you with the temptations you are facing right now!
   b. Pray until you have nothing left to say, then take some time and listen to God.
   c. Read the Scriptures in this chapter on the blood, and apply them to temptation in your life.
   d. Get conversations going with a trusted Christian friend who can help you move forward in your struggle against temptation.
7. Questions worth considering for further study…
   a. Do you have a friend who is a bad influence on you?
   b. Do you have a friend who is a good influence on you?
   c. What kind of an influence are you to others?

8. We live in one of three zones at any given moment.
   a. The first is the *Safety Zone*. This is where your heart is guarded against temptation.
   b. The second is the *Struggle Zone*. This is where the war takes place against temptation. Stay here long enough and you will get hurt.
   c. The third is the *Sin Zone*. You stayed in the Struggle Zone too long.
   d. Discuss which zone you are in and what it would take to move to the *Safety Zone*.

CHAPTER 3

Things to Consider when Trying Something Just Once

I have never accidentally discharged a gun. My brother-in-law is a different story. One day during hunting season he had his gun in the front of the cab and… *kaboom!* He shot a hole right through the floor of the truck. He'd had that gun in his truck a million times before that accident. He is a safe, avid hunter. But on that day, like temptation, the gun went off accidentally because he was careless. This is how temptation oftentimes grabs us; it is when we are careless.

This chapter contains 14 questions I have found helpful in dealing with temptation. They are questions that require further questions. They are questions that require thoughtful reflection and integrity and that will demand answers filled with honesty. They are questions meant to take us away from temptation. They are questions that will help us stop dating temptation. You are invited to use these questions as conversation starters with others.

14 Questions

1. *What if I like the temptation?*

I am sure you will. That is the whole point of temptation; we like it. The reason for discovering our own personal triggers is so we can learn to stay away from potentially dangerous situations. One thing I have learned about shooting a gun is that if you do not put your finger on the trigger, it is far less likely the gun will fire. Further, keep the bullets out of the gun and your finger off the trigger and I am certain the gun will not fire. This is what we need to do with temptation. We need to keep the ammunition away from the gun and keep our finger off the trigger. Short of this, we will fail.

2. *What if I cannot control the temptation?*

You *cannot* control it. Get over it. Our minds fool us and we think we are stronger than what we really are. How many times have we prayed and still messed up? How many times have we quoted Scripture and still messed up? I have prayed and read Scripture and quoted Scripture, but as long as I have a bullet in the gun and my finger on the trigger, I am just fooling myself.

Trying to control temptation is like going to a buffet while on a diet and asking the Lord to give you strength to say no to the temptation. Pray as much as you would like and quote as much Scripture as you would like, in that situation you will fail. Unload the gun and get your finger off the trigger!

What we can control is our behavior before we even put the gun in our hand. That is the point of this book—to help you identify ways you can forecast temptation, so you can go the other direction and stay out of the storm.

I bought a Honda scooter a few years ago when gas hit $4 a gallon. My first time on the scooter was tricky. But after a short while, I mastered the little fellow. Then, as American men do, the next summer I upgraded to a Honda 250 Rebel. My scooter was child's play by comparison. Soon I mastered my Rebel. You guessed it, I upgraded to what I now have—a Honda Shadow 750. Compared to my scooter, this thing is the Empire State Building.

I have to be much more careful with this big guy. Once I get cruising down the road, it roars like a lion. I love the after-market pipes that are on it too. It can look cool, sound cool, and run cool—and it does—but I need to remember I can just as easily dump the thing if I am not careful.

We spend a lot of time in life looking cool and sounding cool. That is when we take a dive with temptation. Control is a fragile possession.

3. *Can the temptation hurt me?*

Pardon me for being so blunt, but that is a stupid question to ask. Of course it will hurt you. That is the reason for staying away from temptation; it hurts…*a lot.*

The reason we mess around with certain temptations we really like is because we have avoided pain to this point. The pleasure of the temptation outweighs the pain in doing the deed. The Bible tells us pleasure will only last for a season.

The consequences of failed temptation will result in disaster, just like a storm. The worst pain I have ever experienced was on October 5, 1991. I was cutting limbs off a tree at my grandma's house. Long story short, a branch fell to the ground, knocking the ladder out from under me. I fell some twenty-four feet to the ground, breaking my back in two places. I had cuts and loss of skin from fingers to armpits. I was a mess.

People would ask me if breaking my back hurt. I really don't understand people some days. It's like those reporters who stick a microphone in a relative's face after a loved one has been killed and ask them how they feel. We know the same is true of failed temptation. It hurts really bad.

4. *What if the temptation replaces something or someone that it should not be replacing?*

That is the problem with temptation—it takes us away from what we should be doing.

Temptation takes away from all the right things and leads us to all the wrong things in life. It leads us to the wrong relationships and replaces good choices with bad choices. It never seems this way at the beginning of the book, but by the time you get into the middle, you begin to see the story is not going to turn out very well. This is why addictions are so dangerous.

5. *Has this temptation caused problems for others?*

Of course it has. You would think we would learn from the mistakes of others. We know this about human nature: we are slow to learn and quick to act and even quicker to react. We somehow think we are different or our situation will be different. That is the lie of temptation. We convince ourselves everything is going to turn out really well. This is a really wrong way to think about temptation.

It may seem like things are going to work out for us even though for others the story turns out to be a disaster. We know we're not really different from everyone else, yet our behavior continues to be destructive. My encouragement to you is to have a reality check with life and learn from all of your temptations of the past. Have any of them worked out when carried out to their completion?

Unload the gun and get your finger off the trigger! I remember a painful Sunday when I was trying to describe personality types. I was describing our youth pastor, who did an awesome job with my kids. As I described him, I said it in a way that really hurt his family. I was devastated the next day when I discovered what I had done. I got in my car and drove to a quiet street and spent the rest of the day crying and praying.

I had hurt someone without realizing what I was doing. This is the way temptation works. We hurt others and, most of the time, are not aware of how much we have hurt them. Always remember that temptation is not as isolated as you may think. It touches a lot of people.

6. *Why am I trying the temptation?*

This is another great question to ask. It is a great one because a lot of the time we just do things without thinking about it, especially when we are with friends.

It has been said that when a teenager is with a friend in the car, their intelligence level is cut by 50%. When you add another friend, the intelligence level is cut yet another 50%, and so on and so forth. In fairness to teenagers, this can be true of all other ages as well.

Good influences produce good results and bad influences produce bad results. We seem to think otherwise some of the time, and those are the times we get ourselves into trouble. We've all been in situations in which we've tried something and, later, don't know why we did.

I do that with food all the time. I'm always trying to push the envelope with hot, spicy food. Thai food is one of my favorite foods. There are times when it is so hot I begin to sweat and tears come to my eyes. My wife looks at me puzzled, wondering why I do this to myself. I never seem to have a very good answer.

This is how we handle temptation sometimes too. There may not be a really good answer as to why we do it. This is yet another reason to begin forecasting temptation so we can do a better job of not giving in to it.

7. *Do I know better?*

Another dumb question, yet a valid one we ignore much of the time. We always know better. I am amused by those who talk about something being amoral. Either it is moral or immoral. Temptation tells us it is uncertain. That is how we convince ourselves to do things we should never do.

I often hear people talk about something being gray. It is either black or white. Temptation wants us to believe things are always a little unclear; therefore, I should walk through that door and deal with the consequences later. This is exactly what I will do: I will deal with the consequences later. The problem with *later* is it always comes.

Once again, I make my point with another food illustration. I love to eat late at night, right before I go to bed. I have been known to have a handful of Hostess cake donuts covered with chocolate for my late-night snack. My favorite ones are the mini donuts, because I convince myself they are smaller and therefore have less of an impact on my gut.

To that I add a glass of milk, then a sandwich and barbecued potato chips. I know better, yet I do it—even though I know exactly how poorly I will sleep and how awful I will feel in the morning. The temptation is to settle for temporary satisfaction without counting the cost. This is temptation in a nutshell.

8. *What is my motive for trying the temptation?*

This is one of the harder questions I ask in this chapter because we do not always try to understand our motives. In other words, what is the main reason I am trying out this temptation? We often use the excuse of curiosity. When dissected a little bit further, we discover it is not so much curiosity as much as it is something much deeper within us.

I am not a psychologist and this book is not a book about psychology; nonetheless, we still need to discover our motives for our behavior. It is a part of learning how to forecast temptation. For me it has a lot to do with my personality. I do things to the extreme, which is also identified in part as what is called *obsessive-compulsive behavior*. I do it with food, with collecting, with relationships. (At least I am consistent and predictable!) Usually our motive has something to do with selfishness. We do what we do because we want to do it. There is something in it for us.

9. Is curiosity dangerous?

This is like asking the devil if he is going to harm us. It may be fun. It may be exciting. It may be fresh. It may be euphoric. It may be the best thing you have ever tried. Bottom line: the devil never ever has our best interest in mind. Of course giving in to temptation will bring harm to our lives. I remember the childhood afternoon when I wanted to see if shooting my foot with a BB gun would hurt. I was wearing tennis shoes and shot my foot. It didn't hurt. So I raised the stakes and shot my bare finger. *That hurt.* Temptation may look like a BB gun, but it can cause the damage of a bazooka.

Forecasting temptation is a great way to troubleshoot and run away from curiosity. Some people are very curious people. Others, like myself, do not have a curious bone in them. I have never thought to shake or open a present ahead of schedule—unlike my wife. During my growing-up years, I was told many times to stay away from something or not do something, and I obeyed. For others, those are words of great challenge. For many people, to be told not to do something means to do just the opposite. Sure, curiosity is dangerous when we are talking about temptation. It is a disaster waiting to happen.

One day before my wife and I were married, we drove over to the

Oregon Coast. Remember, I do not have a curious bone in me, but my wife is quite the opposite. We parked at this cool lookout point where the idea is to enjoy the view from the car. Not my wife. She got out of the car and ran toward the cliff where there were ropes and warning signs. I raced after her and grabbed her from behind, scolding her for getting so close to danger. Even to this day, she still doesn't think she was in danger!

This is the way it is with temptation; curiosity keeps us running to the edge of the cliff, all the while claiming it was never a close call!

10. Does this temptation have a source, or a root, or a relative?
This is another great question that deserves a great answer laced with honesty and some soul-searching.

I've learned that most temptations have a source. What we see at first is just the tip of the iceberg.

I've learned that most temptation has a relative. In fact, now is a good time to introduce you to the seven deadly sins that originate from temptation.

Further, we will see what other types of temptations are related to each one. The seven deadly sins are *pride, greed, envy, anger, lust, gluttony, and sloth*. From these stem all the other sins known to mankind. For these seven deadly sins (as they have been identified throughout history), we can see a connection to their parent: temptation. It gives us better insight into forecasting temptation when we play a particular temptation out to its conclusion.

At this point, a discussion of inversions proves helpful. An inversion is taking the temptation and naming it in its final phase, because that is what sin is. Then taking that identified sin and naming the temptation that leads to that sin.

For instance, take lust as the sin. What could be its inversion in temptation? I suggest that flirting is a viable answer. The inversion then is to say that to flirt is to lust and to lust is to flirt. (Or how about eating donuts at bedtime is gluttony?) This sounds a bit harsh, but it makes the point of the dangers of temptations, where they lead, and the harm they cause. It causes us to look at temptation as no longer harmless but as a potential hurricane, a potential loaded gun with an itchy finger waiting to pull the trigger.

11. What if I need the temptation?

Now we have crossed over into the world of addictions. This is the problem with temptation; it has no intention of stopping at just one event.

The intent of temptation is to get you hooked and ruin your life. The intent of temptation is to turn a single event into many events. By definition, this is an *addiction*. It becomes a way of life; it takes on a life of its own. This is why a package of cigarettes has twenty in it. If it were not an addiction, one would be enough.

A little bit hurts, because it never stops at a little bit. This is what we have to retrain ourselves to think. This can be a game-changer.

This is why the pornography shop has many items in it; nobody stops at just one. And the list goes on and on and on. A purpose of this book is to help us forecast temptation so addictions will never begin in our lives. Yet the words on these pages will help even the most hooked of addicts to move away from their addictions, when they learn to recognize the triggers and teasers that have become "the new normal" in their lives so they can move away from a life of addictions. This is really the process for all of us, addicted or not—getting rid of the triggers and teasers. If you're going to go on a diet, you don't fill your refrigerator with candy bars, soda, ice cream, and other tempting items.

12. What if I am wrong about the temptation and it is harmful to my life? If?

What are you talking about? Temptation, if yielded to, *is* harmful to your life. That is my point. We must stop telling ourselves that a little bit won't hurt. A little bit hurts because it never stops at a little bit. This is what we have to retrain ourselves to think. This can be a game-changer.

I like game-changers in life that are positive. Game-changers are the result of a big event. The biggest event in your life may be to start forecasting your temptations and learn how to run the other way. Notice that I have personalized your temptations. They belong to you. (And mine belong to me.) What you do with them is totally up to you. Nobody else is responsible. You own them. The goal is for them to no longer own you!

January 1st is one of my favorite days of the year. As I am writing this page, it is January 1st and I love the day because it is the excuse I need to make changes. Waiting for dates like this is stupid, but that's the way it is. My doctor mentioned a few months ago that I need to lose a few potatoes. So for the first time in my life, I joined a fitness club. I don't know if I will use my membership, but I have taken the first step.

I am at the age at which time is not on my side. I am chubby, have high cholesterol, and lead a fairly stress-filled life. It just makes sense for me to make an attempt to take better care of myself. I am harming myself by not doing so. Temptation needs to be treated with similar care.

Now is the time to start making a plan against temptation. Make today your January 1. For whatever reason, if in your mind the lightbulb has come on, then this is your January 1. Seize the day!

13. *Is the temptation necessary?*

This is another important question to ask. It's necessary if you think it's necessary. Temptation never needs to be necessary. It becomes necessary when we calendar it into our daily lives, even when we're not aware that we're doing it.

I have a date book in my office for church-related appointments. I have one at home for my personal life also. Many times I don't schedule something, yet it becomes a part of my day. That is the way temptation works. It is rarely ever scheduled; it just shows up and we accommodate it and push other things to the side.

That is how it works with an affair. It's never on the family schedule of events; we simply find a way to make it part of the schedule. It's time we started forecasting these events so they stop ruining our lives.

We have a lot of things in life we think are necessary. We think cell phones are necessary when really they are not. We think soda is necessary when really it is not. We think bottled water is necessary when really it is not. We think organic food is necessary when really it is not. (I know: I have no idea what I am talking about.)

My point is that there are many things we call necessary that are really a luxury, not a necessity. Temptation is not necessary. Stop treating it like you have to have it.

14. Can this temptation in any way have an effect on my eternity?
This final question is more important than any of the thirteen I have already discussed. Yikes! This puts a whole new light on the subject. If I think that, even in the slightest, a temptation could take me away from heaven, then I should try to do my best to stay away from that temptation.

I cannot write the words on this page fast enough because my mind and heart and soul are racing. If it affects your eternity with God, *stay away at all costs.* There is not a single temptation in all of life worth making your friend, if it is going to in any way jeopardize your eternity. Start running the other direction, please!

Some people at this point create theology to accommodate the lifestyle they live. Please do not fall into this trap. Please do not create doctrine that will leave you in a sea of false security.

I make no doctrinal or theological statements in this book, though there are many I could make. Simply stated, this book is not about theology or doctrine. It is a book that acknowledges that we all can mess up and we need to forecast temptation in ways that can help us to be less messed up in the future. I am writing this book because I need it too. I need to be reminded of things I already know. So do you.

I invite you with others to have a conversation about the points brought up in this chapter. I believe we can benefit from taking these silent issues and giving them a voice. There are many forums appropriate for such a conversation.

SCRIPTURES ON POWER

1. Life and death are in the power of the tongue, and those who love it will eat its fruit (Proverbs 18:21).
2. Jesus answered them, "You are deceived, because you don't know the Scriptures or the power of God" (Matthew 22:29).
3. But you will receive power when the Holy Spirit has come upon you, and you will be My witnesses in Jerusalem, in all Judea and Samaria, and to the ends of the earth (Acts 1:8).
4. How God anointed Jesus of Nazareth with the Holy Spirit and with power, and how He went about doing good and curing all who were under the tyranny of the Devil, because God was with Him (Acts 10:38).
5. For I am not ashamed of the gospel, because it is God's power for salvation to everyone who believes, first to the Jew, and also to the Greek (Romans 1:16).
6. But He said to me, "My grace is sufficient for you, for power is perfected in weakness." Therefore I will most gladly boast all the more about my weaknesses, so that Christ's power may reside in me (2 Corinthians 12:9).
7. My goal is to know Him and the power of His resurrection and the fellowship of His sufferings, being conformed to His death, assuming that I will somehow reach the resurrection from among the dead (Philippians 3:10–11).
8. For God has not given us a spirit of fearfulness, but one of power, love, and sound judgment (2 Timothy 1:7).
9. Holding to the form of religion but denying its power. Avoid these people! (2 Timothy 3:5).
10. For His divine power has given us everything required for life and godliness, through the knowledge of Him who called us by His own glory and goodness (2 Peter 1:3).

LESSON #3

1. Genesis 3:1–13. Focus on what the serpent did throughout this passage.
2. Genesis 39:1–23. Focus on what Joseph did throughout this passage.
3. Job1:1–22. Focus on what Job did throughout this passage.
4. Matthew 4:1–11. Focus on what Jesus did throughout this passage.
5. 1 John 2:1–6. Focus on what you can be doing throughout your life based on this passage.
6. What temptations have you faced since we last met as a group? (if applicable)
7. Were you delivered from temptation or did it get you?
8. How were you sucked in to begin with?
9. Are you uncertain about anything as it relates to your struggle with temptation?
10. Help…
    a. What did you do with the Holy Spirit today?
    b. How did you handle your prayer time today?
    c. How will you use the ten verses in this chapter to help you with temptation?
    d. Involve a Christian friend to help you in your battle against temptation.

CHAPTER 4

Forecasting Temptation

In the United States of America, there is an actual hurricane season. I have been in several hurricanes, both in Florida on my way to Haiti and in Haiti itself. On that same trip, we flew over New Orleans right over the top of a hurricane. From that perspective, the hurricane was awesome to see, knowing we were not in any danger. But when our plane landed in Ft. Lauderdale, little did we know that would be one of three hurricanes that would affect our 18-day trip to Haiti.

If there were no damage and if nobody got hurt, hurricanes would be very exciting events and well worth experiencing. The reality is that hurricanes are very damaging and cause a great deal of harm. So does temptation. It is potentially damaging and hurtful. Temptation is a storm we must learn to stay far away from. With a hurricane, there is sometimes a siren that goes off to warn people to take cover. I wish a siren went off every time you and I enter into the eye of temptation. It may seem calm; the reality is that all hell is about to break loose!

We come now to the heart of this book. I believe there are tangible ways to forecast temptation, to see the storm coming before you're caught out in gale-force winds. In this chapter, I identify seventeen ways we can see temptation coming—seventeen sirens to warn us that we're about to encounter temptation. Once you discover the one or two that fit your situation, the goal is to find ways to move away from the temptation. I'm not providing a formula as much as acting as a facilitator who provides you with all the pieces to the puzzle. I want to lay them out in a way that makes it easier for you to put together the puzzle pieces of your life.

17 FACTORS

1. *Loss of focus.*

When we lose our focus in life, whatever the reason, we lose our reason to take the high road. It is a lost focus that causes us to travel roads we otherwise would never travel.

If this is you, I am deeply sorry for the events that have caused you to lose your focus in life. But my focus is on helping you stop the bleeding. Let's not make things worse by adding temptations that will lead to further disaster and destruction. I don't know how to help you find your focus; I am trying to help you to not make things any worse than they already are. I am keenly aware some people reading this book are at a point of total desperation. This is what happens when we lose our focus. We begin to go places we should not go, and the places we wander to are not good for us at all.

If life is a river and we are in a boat, it's time to get the oars back in the water and start rowing. I know the currents of despair are swift, but you have the ability with the power of the Holy Spirit to fight the currents of temptation and move upstream towards the headwaters of peace and purity.

2. *A divided heart.*

A divided heart is a disaster in the making. How do we get divided hearts, and what is the result of a divided heart? We get a divided heart when we get bored with what we have. We begin to look around and realize there are other mountains to climb and other lands to explore.

In other words, the grass is greener on the other side of the fence. The problem is we fail to take a close look at that grass. If we did take a closer look, we'd discover the dog has been in that yard too!

We had neighbors that owned three pit bulls. We have a two-story house, which means we're able to see what goes on in the backyard of our neighbors on either side of us. That is okay, because we know they can see what we do too.

For three years, we watched those dogs do their deed in the backyard. Strange thing about our neighbors was they never cleaned up the yard. Consequently, the dogs eventually created small mountains in the backyard. The neighbors let the grass grow so that it looked like a field, which partly covered the mountains the dogs were creating.

Temptation is like our neighbors' backyard. It begins with one little "mess up," but before you know it there are mountains of messes in our lives, all because we allowed temptation to make those messes in our green grass. If we could live life at a distance, the messes would not be an issue. But life is lived up close and personal, and our feet do travel through the grass. What is in your grass?

3. *Fatigue.*

Fatigue is one of the most devastating avenues to temptation I can name. I used to never give this one any credibility because I prided myself on living on fewer than eight hours of sleep each night. It wasn't until my doctoral program that a professor pointed out the ramifications of inadequate rest.

Of all the things I learned from that program, vulnerability to temptation was perhaps the single most important. Since 2006, I have been religious about getting my rest. And guess what? It has had a direct effect on my temptation level. You heard me right: rest (or rather, the lack thereof) has a direct effect on temptation. What is obvious about a lack of rest besides being grumpy? Our guard is down when we are tired. We do and say some of the dumbest things when we are groggy. It is a little bit like being drunk. Like drunkenness, fatigue will get the best of us, and we will be more vulnerable to temptation than when we are fully rested.

I cannot help but give a bit of advice at this point regarding sleep. Our bodies were made to sleep approximately eight hours or one-third of the day. Think of it: if you live to be seventy-five years old, you have slept away approximately twenty-five years of your life. Why did God create us this way? Who knows? I do know He wants us to glorify Him when we are awake, so the best way I know to do this is to make sure I get adequate rest. Rest directly affects the frequency of temptation in life. (P.S. I'm not saying that if you sleep more than eight hours a day temptation goes away. Sorry, it's not a formula.)

4. *Sin.*

Next is the obvious: sin. If there is sin in our lives that has not been dealt with, we have given temptation the climate necessary to cause hell in our lives. Talk about making a bad problem worse.

If we do not deal with sin in our lives, I can forecast with certainty what our response will be to future temptation. The thinking goes that once we break the rules, why stop with one? The process of thinking clearly becomes clouded with defeatism. We then become self-destructive and do things we would never otherwise do.

It's like deciding to finally start losing weight if you're overweight. The first thing you have to do is to forecast or make a plan. There are three parts to a plan: 1) start; 2) stay the course; and 3) see it through to its conclusion.

I am writing this chapter right after Christmas. Our house is filled with food that will only make me fatter. The forecast is simple. If I do not do something about the food all around our house, I will begin grazing until it is all gone. "Just walk away from it and ignore it," you might say. Honey, it doesn't work that way. The temptation is far too strong. That is why it is in our house to begin with—it tastes so stinking good.

This is how temptation works. Some temptation is easy to forecast. The only way to avoid the temptation is to throw away the food. The only way to avoid further temptation in your life is get rid of the sin!

5. *Compromise.*

Another great forecaster of temptation is in the arena of compromise. I am a political junky. I love the world of politics and law and law enforcement. I understand that in Congress, the only way to legislate is from a position of compromise. Everybody gets a little bit of what they want, but nobody gets everything they want. In Congress, that is a great way to govern. It keeps in play the checks and balances our founding fathers intended us to have.

But when it comes to temptation, compromise is a terrible thing to consider—because a little bit of temptation is a little bit too much. We've heard the phrase regarding our enemies: "We will never negotiate with terrorists."

Well, the same needs to be said about temptation. At all costs, we must avoid negotiating with temptation. Temptation is the enemy! Once we start negotiating we have already given away far too much ground. Compromise will be our demise. Temptation will become our enemy, and we will get hurt.

6. *Your friends.*

I can pretty well forecast temptation in your life by who your friends are. Our peers are the single greatest influence we have in our lives on planet earth. We rarely raise the bar when we are with our friends. We usually lower the bar to the lowest common denominator.

If you have friends who are spiritually strong, you will do better with temptation. But if you have friends who are not spiritually strong, the outcome is very predictable. (Honesty is required here. Most of us think our friends are strong, but that can be part of the problem if it's not really true.)

If I am with people who cuss, I will, at the very least, *think* those same words over a period of time. If I am with people who tell dirty jokes, I will begin thinking about dirty jokes. This is just the way life works. It is not right or wrong, good or bad; it is just the way it is. Our peers influence us more than Jack Daniels at a party gone wild!

7. *Bad attitude.*

This next one has both barrels loaded, and the clip is full. This point covers a garden of weeds that include anger, jealousy, resentment, bitterness, revenge, hate, envy, and pride. If any of these things are at work in your life, guess what? I can forecast a storm heading your way. These add up to a bad attitude.

Temptation loves a bad attitude. Any one of the nasty ways of thinking listed above produces a bad attitude. Stay angry, jealous, or bitter long enough, and you have fertile ground for a bad attitude. And temptations result from bad attitudes. Temptation is looking for an attitude that has gone crazy. When the attitude is out of balance, temptation is lurking just around the corner. Obviously, the key is to do something about the attitude *before* temptation does something with you.

With a bad attitude, you're under its spell—and it's not "love potion number 9," if you know what I mean. The outcome is suicidal. You may have only one bullet in the chamber, but the barrel is pointed at your brain. Sorry for the brutal honesty, but I do not want people thinking temptation is no big deal. It is a huge deal.

8. *Lost hope.*

The first point I mention in this chapter is lost focus. Point #8 is even worse: lost hope. When a person loses hope, life is hard at best. Hope is what keeps people alive. When hope is gone, so is the reason to do what is right. Hopelessness feeds right in to the beast called temptation.

When there is no hope, there is no reason to resist temptation—none at all. This explains a lot of people's behavior. Hope is the single greatest deterrent against temptation. When I have hope, I have a really good reason to do the right thing instead of the wrong thing. And when my hope is in Jesus Christ, I have the highest incentive possible to run the opposite direction of temptation.

Hope is the single greatest deterrent against temptation. When I have hope, I have a really good reason to do the right thing instead of the wrong thing. And when my hope is in Jesus Christ, I have the highest incentive possible to run the opposite direction of temptation.

When hope is lost, though, not only do I do what is wrong, I am likely to seek it out at all costs. This is the destructive nature of hope when it has been lost. The good news is that I have used the word *lost*, not *gone*. Hope that is lost can be found again. As long as we have air in our lungs, hope is never gone; it is simply misplaced. Until hope is rediscovered, forecasting temptation can be accurately made based on hope that is lost.

9. Lack of accountability.

A lack of accountability is a keg of dynamite looking for a blasting cap. If we lack accountability, we certainly are not lacking temptation. This is an example of where the inversion method I spoke of earlier works very well.

If I am lacking in accountability, I am not lacking in temptation. If I am not lacking in accountability, I am lacking in temptation. In other words, each of us needs to be accountable to someone in our lives!

My greatest accountability partner in my life is my wife. I have others too: my friends, my church family, and my peers in the ministry.

My greatest accountability partner is the Holy Spirit. My single greatest human accountability partner is the mirror. I have to look at myself in the mirror every single day. I would definitely act out on a whole lot more temptation if nobody were ever going to hold me accountable, but they are.

Accountability creates a tension in my life. At least I am honest about it. Sometimes temptation wins out and sometimes it does not. The greater the accountability, the greater the likelihood I will walk away from temptation. You will too!

10. A daring spirit.

If you have a daring spirit, I can guarantee you will have a big-time struggle with temptation. Of course, if you have a daring spirit you will also have some great experiences in life too. Likewise, you are likely to have some painful failures as well. I am not a daring person at all. I like vanilla. A daring spirit likes all the flavors. I am content to live in Keizer, Oregon, and except for an occasional trip to New York City, I'm perfectly content to do the same thing day after day because I really like what I do. That is not bad; it's just that it's plain old vanilla.

On the other hand, my wife, Joanie, likes a lot more than vanilla. And she loves to travel. This makes for an interesting marriage. Not a bad one, just interesting. That is for another book, another day.

It is the daring spirit that invites temptation. It is the daring spirit that's willing to try everything and anything just once, and if you like it you'll do it again and again.

The problem with this daring spirit is that temptation becomes far too familiar, and the results can be cataclysmic. A daring spirit is a simple way to forecast temptation. It needs to be noted that a daring spirit is not bad; it is simply a daring spirit that needs tender loving care and attention. Figure out what you are and deal with it accordingly.

11. Lack of convictions.

Another surefire way to forecast temptation is by living with a lack of convictions. This will guarantee that a visit from temptation will come knocking at your door. In fact, I doubt temptation will knock; it will just walk right on into your house. And if your door is locked, temptation will knock your door in, like the vice squad serving a search warrant.

Convictions are nonnegotiable items that do not change with time, culture or circumstances. They are almost as timeless as the Bible because they originate from the Bible. Convictions are the values by which a person's life is governed. Without strong convictions, I have little reason to live a consistent life. Temptation cares little about convictions.

I'll tell you this: if our convictions are to be tested, the testing will come at the hand of temptation. With a lack of conviction, we will likely go to bed with the devil more times than we'd care to admit. We must develop deep convictions that will be the bedrock of our lives on earth. Temptation, when it sees our deep convictions, will not give up on us, but it will recognize that it has been defeated.

12. Isolation.

Isolation is a huge factor in forecasting temptation. Whenever we isolate ourselves from others, we think one-dimensionally. When we isolate ourselves, we are totally removed from the accountability I spoke about earlier in this chapter. It is during our times of isolation that the greatest amount of damage can be done.

When we're in isolation, temptation becomes our own personal category 5 hurricane. It will leave no survivors! Isolation is risky business. It will not be a friend either now or later. Isolation has connections with temptation; e.g., the viewing of Internet pornography. Those two together are a very dangerous combination. They will ruin a life—guaranteed!

As a trained police chaplain I have some limited knowledge in the area of suicide. When notifying a relative of a loved one who has taken his or her own life, the question is often asked why or how the person could do such a thing. Without going into all the responses we give, isolation is at the top of the list. With isolation comes a limited perspective that will lead us down roads we otherwise wouldn't travel. That is the way isolation works in tandem with temptation. Taking your own life becomes the ultimate temptation!

13. Technology.

Exposure to outside influences—namely technology—is a great way to encounter temptation, and it's not hard to forecast these encounters. Need I share with you the statistics on the amount of Internet pornography users in the world? Need I mention how many fathers addicted to pornography on the Internet are sitting in church each Sunday? Need I mention how many pastors who are addicted to Internet pornography are preaching Sunday after Sunday? There are also the temptations to waste time, gossip, and neglect people in our lives because of Internet addictions.

The Internet is but one of many forms of technology available to us in the 21st century. Technology is not going away. Technology is here to stay, and so is temptation. Temptation loves technology. I love technology. I love how easy it is to sit and write a book compared to the days when I was in college and sat on my bed with a manual typewriter in my lap using an eraser pencil to erase every other word. I love being able to communicate with my family when I'm out of town without putting a quarter in the phone before making the call. (Some of you have no idea what I'm talking about.) And the amazing thing of it is that the advancements in technology are accelerating at a rate faster than most of us can keep up with. Technology can be a very good thing.

Temptation, however, is keeping up with technology just fine. In fact, temptation may be the father of technology. Technology is a double-edged sword. Like anything else, it needs to be a tool, not a god.

In many cases, technology is causing shallow relationships even though there has never been so much chatter! Temptation loves meaningless chatter. It becomes a distraction, then an addiction, then it owns us. We are losing our ability to sit face-to-face with another human and have a meaningful conversation. We have forgotten that eyes have color and faces have smiles. We have forgotten that hair is beautiful and dimples are cute.

We are so busy being engulfed by technology that temptation has won this battle too. Overexposure to technology is a definite indicator we can use to forecast temptation.

14. A non-eternal perspective.

A non-eternal perspective is a huge open door to temptation. In fact, if you're living with a non-eternal perspective, you'll have little problem with temptation because like a dirty diaper on a baby—it will follow you wherever you go. That's right, temptation stinks; and you will smell up any room you walk into with a non-eternal perspective.

If there is nothing eternal in your life, then what does it matter ultimately what you do? I teach philosophy and apologetics from a biblical worldview at a local college. A non-eternal view leads to fatalism. In other words, why bother doing what is right if it ultimately doesn't matter? I might as well do what feels best and brings me the most happiness and temporary satisfaction. This is a pathetic way to live life. Even in this state of mind, the storms of temptation will make your life a walking disaster. You can do better—much better.

15. Narcissism and OCD.

We can also forecast temptation for people who are narcissistic and obsessive-compulsive. I know because I have one of these two all of the time and the other some of the time.

Narcissists think only about themselves. One who is obsessive-compulsive lives in a world of extremes. This is me. I am honest. What about you? (Honesty is a great deterrent to temptation.)

For the person who is obsessive-compulsive, if you do it once, you might as well do it again and again. It's like going to a buffet for lunch or dinner—one of my favorite events in all of life. The goal is not to eat well at a buffet; the goal is to eat a lot. I am finished eating at a buffet when I have eaten so much that I physically hurt. The first two plates of food were fun. The third plate of food was a challenge. The fourth plate of food feels like a ruptured appendix. The fifth plate of food resembles death. Yet, I love going to buffets. (I may have exaggerated just a bit—not every plate is full!) That buffet is just like temptation in all areas of life.

Temptation works the same way for the person who is obsessive-compulsive. It takes the idea of it being all about me and adds to it the idea of doing everything in extremes. Therein you have a formula for disaster. A narcissist dives into temptation because it's all about him—he or she is owed. There is a sense of entitlement. So the temptation is not really wrong as much as it is owed. The problem is that the outcome is the same whether you are a narcissist or not. Temptation does not care if you are a narcissist. Temptation only cares that you indulge!

16. Wrong place at the wrong time.

Another easy way to encounter temptation is to be at the wrong place at the wrong time. This one seems almost too easy to forecast, yet it happens enough that I can't ignore it.

How many times do we meet temptation in a place we do not belong doing something with someone we never planned to do something with in the first place? There are quite a few people sitting in jail who fit this description. There are a lot of lonely, miserable people who fit this description.

I could give a sermon on making wise choices, but it would fall on deaf ears. Temptation has a way of giving us directions to the wrong place at the wrong time so we might do the things we shouldn't do. You might say temptation is our GPS to trouble.

17. Giving the enemy a platform.

This last item is our ability to give the enemy a platform. The enemy in this case is temptation. We are far too nice when it comes to temptation. Temptation is not to be tolerated.

I know we live in a day when tolerance is what matters most if we want to be any kind of a person at all. Temptation loves tolerance. Tolerance tolerates temptation. The goal of this book is to help us dethrone temptation. Take temptation off the pedestal you have placed it on. Temptation gets enough attention without our placing it on a pedestal. We'll never be able to kill temptation, but we can do our best to wound it! We tolerate it only because we have no choice.

Scriptures on Need

1. Don't be like them, because your Father knows the things you need before you ask Him (Matthew 6:8).
2. But when He heard this, He said, "Those who are well don't need a doctor, but the sick do. Go and learn what this means: I desire mercy and not sacrifice. For I didn't come to call the righteous, but sinners" (Matthew 9:12–13).
3. When the crowds found out, they followed Him. He welcomed them, spoke to them about the kingdom of God, and cured those who needed healing (Luke 9:11).
4. So the eye cannot say to the hand, "I don't need you!" nor again the head to the feet, "I don't need you!" On the contrary, all the more, those parts of the body that seem to be weaker are necessary (1 Corinthians 12:21–22).
5. But our presentable parts have no need of clothing. Instead, God has put the body together, giving greater honor to the less honorable, so that there would be no division in the body, but that

the members would have the same concern for each other (1 Corinthians 12:24–25).

6. If boasting is necessary, I will boast about my weaknesses (2 Corinthians 11:30).
7. And my God will supply all your needs according to His riches in glory in Christ Jesus. Now to our God and Father be glory forever and ever. Amen (Philippians 4:19–20).
8. Therefore let us approach the throne of grace with boldness, so that we may receive mercy and find grace to help us at the proper time (Hebrews 4:16).
9. For though by this time you ought to be teachers, you need someone to teach you again the basic principles of God's revelation. You need milk, not solid food. Now everyone who lives on milk is inexperienced with the message about righteousness, because he is an infant. But solid food is for the mature—for those whose senses have been trained to distinguish between good and evil (Hebrews 5:12–14).
10. For you need endurance, so that after you have done God's will, you may receive what was promised (Hebrews 10:36).

LESSON #4

1. Genesis 3:1–13. Talk about unhealthy conversations that lead us down the wrong roads in life.
2. Genesis 39:1–23. Talk about unhealthy living environments that take us down the wrong roads in life.
3. Job 1:1–22. Talk about unhealthy circumstances that may be beyond our control that lead us astray.
4. Matthew 4:1–11. Talk about healthy conversations that keep us on the straight and narrow.
5. 1 John 2:1–6. Talk about beliefs that are in reality unhealthy because they lead to temptation.
6. Forecasting temptation…
    a. Identify your weaknesses including your single greatest weakness.

b. Identify your most common temptation.
c. Identify your pattern of behavior associated with your most common temptation.
d. Identify your spiritual victories.
e. Identify your needs today as they relate to temptation.

7. Help…
   a. What have you done with the Holy Spirit today?
   b. Are you prayed up? If you don't know what I mean by this, you are not prayed up! Time, time, time is the key!
   c. Are you read up? If you don't know what I mean by this, you are not read up! Time, time, time is the key!
   d. Who is helping you with your temptations?

CHAPTER 5

QUESTIONS TO ASK ABOUT TEMPTATION

Guns can be very dangerous and need to be treated as though they are always loaded. It's always the "unloaded" gun that makes such horrific accidents in life. The stories on the news are always the same. We're always surprised to discover the gun was loaded and we did not know it. Temptation is more than a smoking gun. It is a loaded gun; and it is pointed at you. We must do better at recognizing that, or temptation is going to blow us away.

In chapter 3, we look at questions to ask about temptation itself, about its nature and how it might affect us. The point was to see temptation and its consequences in an honest way. This chapter asks more questions that are closely related to temptation, questions that get even more up close and personal. I hope these questions will unmask temptation in your life and make you hate it—that they will prove to you that the gun is loaded.

My goal is not to provide you with answers so much as bring up the questions so you can come up with your own answers. (However, I will give some answers where I absolutely cannot contain myself.)

26 QUESTIONS

1. *What is my motivation for yielding to this particular temptation?*

This is a great question to ask. In other words, why am I considering this temptation? "I don't know" is not a valid answer, though it is the one most commonly given. If you don't know why you do the things you do, I encourage you to figure it out.

Temptation does not want you to figure it out because then it will have less of a hold on your life. Why *do* we do the things we do? Sometimes there are a few good answers and sometimes our answers stink. Figure out the motive, and you may be able to better tame temptation in your life.

2. *Will the temptation I am about to indulge in lead to sin in my life?*

If so, should that make any difference? I love this line of questioning because it is analytical in nature. I love to analyze this kind of stuff because it helps me understand why we do the things we do. It helps me to understand why I do the things I do.

Some temptations may not lead to sin. Most of them probably do. For instance, if I'm tempted to read my Bible that certainly isn't going to lead to sin. Or if I'm tempted to buy roses for my wife, that certainly will not lead to sin. But if I buy my wife's best friend roses it might be a good time to check out the motive, because chances are those roses should be going to my wife—not her good-looking best friend!

You'd think it would be a no-brainer to realize that if a temptation leads to sin, we would stay clear of that temptation. That is generally not how it works. In fact, it seems to work in quite the opposite way. If it leads to sin, somehow the temptation is stronger and more desirable. That is very unfortunate!

3. *Is there a chance the temptation I am considering could become an addiction in my life?*

If anything I do becomes an addiction as a result of repeated temptation, is that something I should take a second look at? Probably so.

Therefore, I should understand the nature of the kinds of temptations I feel myself drawn to. There will probably be a pattern. Temptation never wants us to think that any temptation will lead to an addiction. But remember: temptation is a big fat liar. If my temptation looks like someone else's addiction, there is a really good chance it will become an addiction in my life as well. Yikes!

4. *Is there a chance my temptation will harm someone else?*

Ultimately, the answer is yes on this for every temptation. It is very difficult to find a temptation that doesn't deliver on this promise. It is one thing for me to indulge in temptations of my choosing. But if I am aware it can hurt someone else, then that is more than selfish of me—it is just plain stupid!

So many people have been hurt by another person's temptation. We call this fallout normal. The problem is that our senses have become so dulled we no longer recognize the poison as poison.

One is too many if my temptation is harmful to another human being, especially someone I love. Far too many people are being hurt by the actions of others who are close to them. We live in a very cruel and selfish world. I fear temptation has a death grip on many people. Forecasting our temptation is an attempt to move away from the grip that temptation has on all of us!

5. *How will giving in to this temptation impact my children, my family, my job?*

This question is considerably more specific than the previous question. I really do not want to address this question, but I must for all the children who are victims, for all the employers who have had to fire someone because of the employee's selfish stupidity, and for every spouse who has had to live with the shame of a spouse who chose to go to bed with temptation instead of family.

On the other hand, I am keenly aware that most people, when tempted, do not take time to think about who it will hurt. We never take time to figure out if it's a good thing for everyone concerned. The trance that temptation puts people in—people who are otherwise very intelligent—is simply amazing.

How many more children must be abandoned before we get aggressive with this beast we call temptation? How many more careers must be flushed down the toilet due to temptation gone wild? I hope that by now all of us are looking at temptation differently. Hopefully it is beginning to smell. Hopefully it is beginning to turn our stomachs inside out. Hopefully it is giving you a new determination to take on temptation with a vengeance.

6. *Where did the temptation originate?*

This is a fascinating question for us to consider. It is fascinating because everything has a source. If you can find the source, you might be able to find a remedy for the disease. Yes, temptation is a disease. It is a cancer; it is ugly, and it is deadly. I want all of us to want a cure for the disease. I want all of us to want a cure for this cancer. And I want us to take off the Cinderella mask and see temptation for what it really is: Godzilla!

If you can find the source, you might be able to find a remedy for the disease. Yes, temptation is a disease. It is a cancer; it is ugly, and it is deadly.

I remember a family trip when I was in high school. One of my memories of that trip was going to the head of a river. It was not a very big stream, but it was where the river had its origin. The small bubble of water coming out of the ground did not seem very significant unless you followed it downstream to where it became a mighty rushing river.

This is the way temptation begins. It starts with a small stream and before you know it turns in to a might rushing river of destruction!

Temptation always leaves a smoking gun trail. Temptation has nothing new to offer. Temptation always has a source. Discover the source and you might be able to head temptation off at the pass. Ignore the source and "Katie, bar the doors!" Turn out the lights; the party will indeed be over. You might even start to hear the fat lady sing!

7. *Is the temptation I am about to embrace healthy?*

This is a tough question to evaluate because it is a tough answer to prove. Some things are obviously unhealthy. Other things are harder to discern.

In other words, the verdict is out on Twinkies still. From all the research I find in my cupboards, I cannot yet determine if Twinkies are unhealthy. How stupid is that? Of course Twinkies are unhealthy! Anything that has a reported shelf life of 25 years can't be good for you if it's in the food family. (But, hey, at my age, I need all the preservatives I can get!)

The truth of the matter is that temptation isn't healthy. It is harmful, and it will never be your friend. It is the Twinkie in the corner!

8. *If I indulge in the temptation I am so eager to consider, is that mostly smart or mostly stupid?*

I love this question because I do best with things that are obvious. I do well when I have only two choices to make. In fact, I do even better when there's only one choice to make. In fact, I do my best when there are no choices and the decision is made for me. Question #8 can be understood by a child. (Temptation is not rocket science.)

Forecasting temptation isn't about something that is difficult; rather, it's about something that is simple that we have made difficult. Life gets complicated when we get into bed with temptation. The more time we spend with temptation, the more difficult life becomes.

Question #8 asks if the temptation I am so eager to consider is mostly smart or mostly stupid if I do it. Now you know why I love the question. Is it smart or stupid?

9. *What is the financial cost of this temptation I am so in love with?*

Either directly or indirectly, there is a financial cost to temptation. I am a cheapskate. (At least that is the evaluation pronounced by my wife, my family, my friends, my acquaintances, my neighbors, my church family, etc.) There is overwhelming evidence that I cannot ignore; I am cheap. Therefore, the temptations I choose do not cost me much financially—directly, that is.

However, as I stated, all temptation has a cost, so let's not fool ourselves here. Some people spend lots of money on their temptations of choice. So they—maybe you—are paying twice. They pay both directly and indirectly. Even if we can financially afford our vice of choice, the truth is that no matter how much money we have in the bank, giving in to this temptation will bankrupt us one way or the other.

Being able to afford temptation financially misses the point. Temptation goes beyond a monetary value. Temptation is priceless. It takes everything you have and more. Temptation is greedy and will not stop until it has all of you.

When you go to a fancy restaurant and there are no prices listed on the menu, you know the prices are high. Temptation is that way. It has no price tag on it; just know it costs more than what you have in your pocket!

10. How will temptation affect my integrity and reputation?

I spend time during my week with cops in their cars while on patrol. That is part of what I do as a police chaplain. After hearing a lame response from a suspect, one cop said, “Really?” to the guy—meaning “is that the best you can come up with?”

How will temptation affect my integrity and reputation? Really? If you have to ask the question, I guess temptation has the best of you. Temptation is *never* good for a reputation or for integrity. In fact, temptation is no friend of integrity and reputation. This bus has room for two and no more. Temptation needs to find another ride!

11. Is it legal?

That's a novel question to ask. Some temptations are very illegal. One would think that would be reason enough to stay away from the temptation. It's as if our brains are turned off when it comes to the trance of temptation.

I live in the meth capital of the United States per capita. Meth is lurking throughout our city. I see meth addicts and their victims on a regular basis. I remember one day when I was doing a ride-along with a cop who had pulled over a suspect. The officer suspected meth use. After several denials, the driver confessed to meth use but she said she had not done if for days. After a legal search of her body, the officer still suspected meth evidence on her. After several questions from the officer, she confessed to stuffing the pipe down her pants somewhere near Australia! I watched her go down under and pull it out. It was gross. It was illegal. It was stupid. It began with temptation!

12. Is the temptation I am considering more right or more wrong?
This question is very different from asking whether it is right or wrong. This question addresses something that will help us to better forecast an approaching storm.

We sometimes make excuses for temptations that we declare as not being wrong. That does not mean they are right, but it does mean they are not wrong. But when you ask the question, “Is it possible for the temptation to lean toward wrong and away from right?” the answer is more times than not yes.

This may be a more helpful way to address temptation than with just black-and-white language. Please note that the question is still black and white. It just helps us to get where we need to go in a more efficient fashion.

13. How will the temptation affect my life?
This is a big-picture question. Be careful with this one. It’s easy to answer that the temptation will have a small impact on my life. The problem is a bunch of smalls equal a biggie! All temptation affects all of life, seen or unseen. Please take my word for it. And it will always affect one’s life adversely unless halted and used as a reminder of what once was.

Too many times, people live with regrets in life. I teach a college Bible study at my church one night a week. I have done this since 2000 with the exception of about two years when our church hired a college pastor. I am back doing it again and love it. The motive in teaching this Bible study is to help my young friends make it through the college years up to age 30 with as few scars as possible.

Temptation creates scars. Scars were once open wounds that were extremely painful. My goal is to limit the number of scars young people get during those years of vulnerability. You limit the scars by how you deal with temptation. Temptations are scar-makers. How will this temptation affect my life? My life will be affected with scars that will serve as a reminder of just how nasty temptation really is.

14. Why am I doing it?

This is the $64,000 question. There is usually one of two answers when we boil down all the other answers. One: "I don't know why I did it." This one is so lame I don't even count it.

The second answer is an answer that is true of all temptation to one degree or another. That answer would be: "Because it felt good." Isn't that the bottom line? This is the essence of hedonism, which says, "If it feels good, do it." It's really the essence of humanity. We do the things that feel good. To do otherwise goes against common sense, except for the person who finds pleasure in pain. (Let's not even go there.)

I do the things I do because in some way they bring me pleasure, even if for a fraction of a second. This is the essence of temptation. Temptation is all about pleasure. It's all about short-term pleasure that creates lasting pain. I argue that it is misplaced pleasure. Surely there are other sources for pleasure outside of temptation. In fact, I will go so far as to say it is a generic pleasure that never has the ability to become the real deal.

How sad that for so many we settle for leftover mashed potatoes. We settle for Spam when we could enjoy a king's prime rib. This is the nature of temptation; at first appearance it looks like prime rib, but it tastes like Spam. When it comes out in the light, it isn't even bad dog food!

15. How does this temptation make me a better or a happier person?

This question comes at temptation from a different direction. In the short run there is often happiness, but in the long run there is not much happiness when we do it over and over again.

Temptation, if repeated over and over, never makes us better.

Temptation usually makes us bitter, not better. This is the nature of temptation. To say that temptation makes me better and happier is to live a lie. It only makes me better and happier if I don't do it!

16. Is the temptation something that will affect my relationship with God?
If question #14 is the $64,000 question, this question is that times ten! The bottom line question for a Christian ought to be: "Will this make my relationship with God better or worse?"

Temptation, when yielded to, never makes my life with God better. In fact, each and every time temptation wins out, God has to go to the blood bank and get out another quart of blood that came from the cross and apply it to my actions. Thank God for a blood bank that never runs dry. And thank God for grace that covers my sin.

But let's not use this blood bank in a way that makes temptation look like a good thing. My goal is to use as little of this blood as I have to. Why? I have already used a bunch of blood, and unfortunately I will probably need some more blood before this book gets published. And I know I will need it well into the future. The goal here is to use less and less the longer we walk with God. Less temptation means the need for less blood!

17. Is the temptation something I need to hide from other people?
Of course it is. If it is something you are proud of, then you're free-falling over the cliff to the rocks below. You're probably dragging friends over the cliff with you as well. The very nature of temptation is that it is secretive.

That fact that temptation is secretive is the very reason for writing this book. It is to get the subject out in the open where it can be eaten one bite at a time. It is the only way I know how to eat an elephant. Temptation is the elephant in the room. We need to have a healthy discussion on temptation because it is destroying lives. We need to learn the triggers that are in our lives and the teasers that get the best of us. Then we can learn to forecast temptation so we can become conquerors and overcomers in the Lord Jesus Christ!

18. Ten years from now, will I be glad I did it?

As it relates to temptation, this is an important question. It goes to the issue of regret and wishing I would have lived life differently. It allows me to look into my future and forecast my future based on my actions of today.

I challenge all of us to look at the temptation that marks our lives today and ask question #18, which really is a theoretical question. It really is only a question of theory, since nobody knows for sure how what we do today will affect life in the future, much less ten years from now.

But consider this scenario: Suppose I have an affair. I presume I will lose my job. The first book I wrote on relationships will get flushed down the toilet. (At least it should.) This book becomes a curse. My life with my wife will be forever messed up as well as my relationship with my family. My opportunity to earn income as I know it will be wiped away and many children who have watched me as their pastor will be eternally damaged. These are just a few of the ripples that would come as a result of an affair. So you tell me, is it worth it?

If we were to ask Rockefeller question #18, he would probably answer no. The grandson of the oil baron John D. Rockefeller, Nelson made a run for the presidency against Barry Goldwater in 1964. It all came down to the California primary. Whoever won in California would clinch the Republican nomination for president.

The weekend before the convention, Rockefeller's 36-year-old wife gave birth to their son. (Rockefeller had previously divorced his wife of more than 30 years and married his mistress.) He suspended his campaign over the weekend to go home and be with his wife and their new son. Goldwater capitalized on this and won the California primary and eventually the Republican nomination.

The one thing the Rockefellers have not achieved in American life was the White House. Ten years from now, will I be glad I did what I am doing today in relation to my temptation?

19. Is this temptation connected to anything else in my life?

Sometimes the reason I do the things I do is because there is a connection between my temptation and another area of my life. I'm not sure what you will make of this question and how you can relate it to your situation, but given time, you will see the connection.

Everything is related to something. Nothing stands alone on its own. Every temptation we face is related to something else in our life. Life is a series of events that are connected to one another. We are all connected to one another too. My temptation is in some way connected to somebody else's temptation and so on.

Temptation is not kept in a box that is isolated from the rest of life. The key is for us to find the connections in our lives. This exercise will help us discover more of the nature of our temptation. Temptation doesn't want us to know these things, but then again temptation is not in charge. Right?

20. With my temptation, do I have eternity in mind?

We need to live our lives in light of eternity. Anything short of this perspective and temptation will be bigger in our lives than it needs to be.

If I am truly thinking about eternity, I will think twice before doing something that has no eternal value. At least this is the way I think it should work. My challenge to you is to give this question some thought in light of two things: your eternity and your temptation.

21. Is my temptation something that will make society better?

This is a great question to ask for all those who feel we live in a community. It is also a great question to ask for all my postmodern friends who believe there is no such thing as individuality and that all things are shared within the community. We move, act, think, live, and breathe in community. If this is true, then all the more reason to give this question careful consideration.

The long and the short of it is that temptation never makes a community better. If temptation makes the individual worse off, it's bound to make society worse too. If it makes society worse, it is bound to make the individual worse. Again, I am using the inversion method to see through this dilemma in order to gain an accurate perspective. Temptation does not make society better!

22. *What does the Bible say about my temptation?*

Yikes! The 800-pound gorilla just walked into the room. What does the Bible say? Talk about taking the wind out of the sails. If it is a temptation, then the Bible has something to say about it.

The Bible addresses temptation specifically and generally. In the Bible there is universal revelation and particular revelation. Unfortunately for temptation, the Bible clobbers it on both sides of the head. The one who says the Bible is silent on temptation is the one who is controlled by temptation. The beast has won if this is the conclusion of the matter. My dilemma is getting you the reader to better know what the Bible says about temptation.

This book is an attempt to talk about temptation from my view, which comes from a biblical perspective. If you find agreement with what I am saying, you will find agreement with the Scriptures too. I care much more that you agree with the Bible than with me. Ultimately, what I say isn't worth a plugged nickel. What the Bible has to say is priceless.

Temptation starts running in fear when people start reading their Bibles. They will discover temptation is a liar and a thief and has robbed many a good person of their joy and their life and their livelihood. The Bible says temptation is a thief. I was taught as a little boy to stay away from people like that. What about you?

23. *When in my life did I first give this temptation a thought, and what was life like before I gave temptation my devotion?*

I can answer the second part of this question with ease.

Before I knew much about temptation my devotional life was better. There is no other way to slice that piece of bread. Innocence is priceless! When did I first start courting temptation? Great question to ask, because chances are it will explain a whole lot of other things in my life as well.

Doing something for the first time gets a lot of attention. The first night of my honeymoon was a big deal; I was in my 20s. The first time I was a pastor of a larger church it was a big deal; I was in my 30s. The first time I got straight As was a big deal; I was in my 40s. The first time I rode a motorcycle it was a big deal; I was in my 50s. (By the way, I own the most gorgeous Honda Shadow 750 you've ever seen. It has more chrome than my first car—a '54 Chevrolet. It has pipes that roar louder than my wife telling me to take out the garbage. It is an awesome bike. Most people going through a midlife crisis think that way about their bikes!) But I didn't just quit doing any of these things after that first time.

So it is with temptation. There is always a first, but there is something about temptation that keeps us coming back for more. Figure that out and we are halfway home!

24. How long have I had this temptation in my head?

The answer to this question is about 18 inches lower than the head. If it is in my head, it is only because I have given it a place in my heart. That's right: Temptation is a heart issue. Get the heart right and you will get temptation right.

We need look no further than that place in our body where love and devotion find its roots—the heart. Deal with the heart and you can deal with temptation. Ignore the need of the heart and temptation will devour you!

25. How will temptation affect my relationship with Jesus Christ?

Jesus is my best friend. I trust He is your best friend too or you probably would not have read this far in this book. You care about your relationship with Jesus Christ so you care about handling temptation.

Temptation has a direct impact on my relationship with Jesus Christ. Because I love Him, there is no room to love temptation. Both demand my all. One died for me: Jesus. The other wants me dead: temptation. My desire to serve Jesus over temptation is a simple choice to make. Yet, how come there are some moments when I don't live that way? It's very frustrating. Either way, what I do with temptation directly affects my relationship with Jesus Christ.

26. *If everyone approached temptation the way I approach it, what would the world be like?*

I have always asked these kinds of "it really doesn't matter" sort of questions. Yet, it is possible that on this subject it just might matter—maybe.

This chapter has pushed you to ask some hard questions about temptation in your life. We need to find some conclusions and solutions as well. I'll offer mine in the final chapter of this book. Until then, I invite you to grab another Twinkie and read on. The next chapter is sure to raise a few eyebrows!

SCRIPTURES ON FAITH

1. But Jesus turned and saw her. "Have courage, daughter," He said. "Your faith has made you well" (Matthew 9:22).
2. And He said to the woman, "Your faith has saved you. Go in peace" (Luke 7:50).
3. So faith comes from what is heard, and what is heard comes through the message about Christ (Romans 10:17).
4. Be alert, stand firm in the faith, be brave and strong (1 Corinthians 16:13).
5. For we walk by faith, not by sight (2 Corinthians 5:7).
6. Now it is clear that no one is justified before God by the law, because the righteous will live by faith (Galatians 3:11).
7. In every situation take the shield of faith, and with it you will be able to extinguish the flaming arrows of the evil one (Ephesians 6:16).
8. Fight the good fight for the faith; take hold of eternal life, to which you were called and have made a good confession before many witnesses (1 Timothy 6:12).
9. I have fought the good fight, I have finished the race, I have kept the faith (2 Timothy 4:7).
10. Now faith is the reality of what is hoped for, the proof of what is not seen (Hebrews 11:1).

LESSON #5

1. Hebrews 11:1–40. Read the entire chapter. Below are four types of faith. Identify which one best fits you and which one you most would like to possess. Discuss.
    a. A young faith… Childhood conversion
    b. A church faith… It has always been expected of me.
    c. A discovered faith… Everything is new and fresh and exciting and awesome.
    d. A disciplined faith… I regularly experience the presence of I AM in my soul.
2. Further helps in combating temptation …
    a. Read large volumes of Scripture.
    b. Go extended periods of time without eating for purposes of inner healing and cleansing of your soul.
    c. Spend a large block of time in prayer.
3. Helps …
    a. What have you done with the Holy Spirit today?
    b. Are you prayed up today?
    c. Are you read up in Scripture today?
    d. Who is sharpening you?

CHAPTER 6

THE LIST

Storms are a part of nature and they are a part of life. Just when you think everything is calm, here comes a cyclone nobody saw coming. It seems to me there are more and more major weather events happening in the world and especially in the Unites States. Likewise, it seems like there are a lot of storms brewing in people's lives. Perhaps we as church leaders have not equipped people with the tools needed to plow through the fields of this century. I trust this book will help break up the fallow ground that is before you.

I feel like I might alienate some readers in this chapter. However, my intent is to continue the conversation, even if it hurts. Remember, this is not a book on sin; it is a book on temptation. So while I'm not passing judgment, I will not shy away from addressing temptations I see and calling them out for the sins they lead to. The following 24 items are areas that I consider tempting, therefore things that are a temptation. It makes perfect sense to me; hopefully it will to you.

As you read, I invite you to enter this conversation with me and consider how these temptations can shape our lives and the lives of society as well. With each of the 24 I will make a statement that could be controversial; yet there will be some who will agree. The point is that these areas of life are life-changers. Therefore, consider carefully how you approach them.

At the very least they are temptations. At the very most they are sin. Either way, they have caused harm to relationships. Remember, temptation is a storm seeking to destroy whomever it can. It is a loaded gun pointed at your life. Temptation is not a game. Temptation takes no prisoners alive. Be careful!

24 TEMPTATIONS

1. *Flirting.*

Flirting is not just "being friendly." Keep your eyes and hands and mind off people you are not married to. If you are single, flirting with another unmarried person is permissible and even encouraged. This is how the game is played. But once you are married, the only person you ever flirt with again is your spouse.

Every extramarital affair begins with flirting. It's fun and addicting and a very dangerous game to play. It shows what's in the heart when you flirt with someone other than your spouse. If that's where you're living right now, take it as a sign that you're messed up and it's time to get things right in the relationships that matter the most: the one with God and the one with your spouse!

2. *Alcohol.*

We call this temptation culturally acceptable in the church these days. That's fine if that's the game you want to play. However, it is still a temptation. I've been on far too many calls to be a fan of alcohol. I've seen its effects when working with the police. I've seen its effects when counseling families from my church. I conducted a funeral for a young mother who was killed in a car accident by a person who had been drinking alcohol. Her eight-month-old baby in her womb died too.

You'll never convince me that alcohol has added value to our culture. In my world it has caused far more harm than good. If you're a parent of a young child, are you counting the days until you can teach your child how to drink? If you are, you need to get help real quick because that is crazy thinking! In all my years of pastoral care, I've never heard anyone tell me alcohol was the answer to a broken relationship. Alcohol is not the answer to anything. Alcohol is a temptation that leads to a lot of heartache!

3. Smoking.

Smoking is a temptation. It starts out as curiosity. I can't think of another reason why a person would start smoking. Today a pack of cigarettes is quite expensive. They provide no food value. Cigarettes stink really bad. They are really bad for you. They show the power of temptation.

Truth be told, smoking is one of the stupidest things in the world to do. Smoking is a great example of how manipulative temptation is. Temptation says to us that smoking is cool and fun. What a crock from the pit of hell. It's a great lesson to us about how deceptive temptation is. If temptation can get us to smoke, imagine what else it can get us to do that makes no sense at all!

4. Chewing tobacco.

I have a fair number of friends who chew tobacco. Chewing tobacco is gross and it creates cancer too! It's as if some days when temptation comes knocking at our door we have no brain whatsoever.

Professional baseball players and others who are looked up to in our culture by our children should be ashamed of themselves for leading our children down a path that is gross, sick and harmful to their health.

I'm reminded of a man who attended our church for a season. He was a horse-racing guy. He came one Wednesday night to a class I taught at the church. I suppose there were about 100 people attending the class. He brought his Bible and a can to class. I wondered what the can was for until he spit the first gross chunk of saliva out of his mouth mixed with dark residue from the wad he had in his mouth. He did this the entire evening.

He started attending on Sundays too. Yep. He did the same thing in church as well. I was glad he came and never scolded him or asked him to stop. His soul was too precious to me. That may surprise you given the language I use on this temptation. I hate chewing tobacco, but I love people! I'm not sure I know what Jesus would have done; I simply told you what I did.

5. *Marijuana.*

Yeah, I listed this as a temptation. I live in Oregon where marijuana comes up on the ballot often enough that I suppose one day it will be legal. Marijuana is a temptation. It highlights the problem with temptation: deception. Advocates convince society that something is helpful rather than harmful.

Temptation will not stop with marijuana. It will continue to convince people that something else needs to be legalized as well and that something else needs to be legalized. Before you know it, there will be nothing left that is illegal. The issue is not whether or not it's legal. The issue remains, is it a temptation? It is a temptation that causes a lot of harm to our society.

Do you want your children smoking pot? I didn't think so. If you answered yes then probably your favorite song is "Puff the Magic Dragon." You probably drive a Volkswagen van from the 60s, your clothes are a little weird and your theme for life is "flower power." Marijuana is a dangerous temptation!

6. *Gambling.*

In our state it's called gaming. Call it whatever you want, it is a temptation.

I remember the Sunday morning a man whom I had never seen before walked into our sanctuary long before it was time for church to begin. He looked like he had been up all night (because he had been up all night). We went through the morning order of service, and when church was over he just sat there in the row acting as though he had nothing to live for.

At that time one of our first casinos in Oregon had just opened about 30 minutes from our church. This man had been there just hours before spending his entire night gambling. He gambled away everything he owned and did not know how to tell his wife. He came to church, sat down, and had every intention of ending his life. Yes, gambling is a temptation. It's fun, and it's exciting, and it's addicting, and it's entertaining, and it's temptation. It's a good one to stay away from!

If you love the money part of it, get a second job and earn it the honest way. If it's not about the money, then play at home without any money involved.

When I was on a cruise, I went to the casino to watch people gamble. I took a mental pad and pencil and played the games behind some of the gamblers, keeping track of how much I would have won or lost. That was just as much fun as gambling. In fact, because I lost (on paper), it was more fun because I never lost a dime. By the way, Las Vegas was not built on winners! Temptation loves to gamble. Stay away from it!

7. *Pornography.*

Pornography is a temptation. I'm not sure how much I need to say on this temptation. It should be fairly self-explanatory. It amazes me that people have created degrees of pornography. The most deceiving category is "soft porn." It makes it sound like this is the one for beginners and Christians.

Porn is porn is porn. It is all bad. It is addicting and controlling and has ruined millions of lives. Apply here what I wrote in a previous chapter about discovering the roots of a temptation. Where did pornography begin for you? For most little boys who grew up in America before the Internet was invented (by Al Gore), it began with the Sears catalog and "I Dream of Jeannie" and "Gilligan's Island." If you don't know what I mean, then never mind. If you know what I mean, then you know what I mean. Either way, pornography starts small.

I saw a centerfold when I was in college because someone showed it to me before I realized what he was about to show me. Unfortunately, I have never forgotten that event. Pornography works that way. Pornography is a major temptation. Stay far away from it.

MOST FREQUENT TEMPTATIONS*

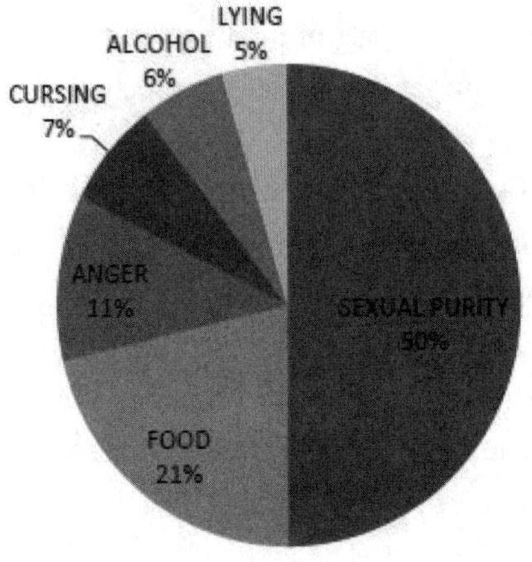

*See Appendix: Surveying Temptation

8. *Cursing.*

Cussing. Swearing. Call it whatever you like; it is a temptation. I've never really had a problem with this temptation. When I was younger my dad taught me a word to say whenever I got really mad. He first encouraged me not to ever get really mad. But if I got really mad, I was to use a word in place of swearing. The word he taught me to use was "horsefeathers." I have no idea what it means. I've never asked my dad what it means. It probably doesn't mean anything. Imagine being at school, getting angry and letting that one rip! Well, that is exactly what I did and still have been known to say it from time to time.

Swearing is unappealing, foul, and not necessary. It impresses the wrong people and only hurts the one who is swearing and likely embarrasses the ones we love the most. It's very habit-forming too. I work with the police department on a regular basis, and the language sometimes is not exactly church language. It's awful to admit, but if you spend enough time around people who swear, those words will come to your mind when they shouldn't be in your mind at all. Swearing is definitely a temptation and extremely habit-forming. Guard your mind and your tongue and your heart.

9. Prescription drugs.

Please hear me out on this before you shoot me. It was just released in December of 2010 that one out of every four children is on some sort of regular prescription drug. I'm not a doctor or a psychologist, but I know there's a need for drugs when the situation warrants it. My concern is for those who have the temptation to take prescription drugs as an acceptable way of coping with life when in fact they become an unnecessary addiction as adults.

I have in fact counseled people in my church who have testified to the very strong temptation of continuing prescription drugs when there was no longer a medical reason to take them. If you're in this category, then this point of temptation is very real. If this does not apply to you, then relax; another shoe is sure to fit your foot!

The temptation to take prescription drugs in this country is a way of life. Everyone's doing it, right? It used to be that prescription drugs were the exception; now they are the rule. I had surgery earlier this year and was prescribed Vicodin. I know for some it is a wonderful drug. For me it was absolutely terrible. I did stuff I didn't know I was capable of doing. After one day of taking this drug, I stopped taking it. I didn't want to become reliant on the part of them that made me goofy! (I'm goofy enough without any help!)

My point is simple: for quite a few people, prescription drugs are a temptation because they take away something you don't want to feel or confront. Be careful with this temptation; lots of people have been hurt by it.

10. Adultery.

That's right, the big scarlet "A." This is one time you don't want to have an "A." To say adultery is a temptation would be a gross understatement. Nonetheless, among other things that is what it is.

We need to have an honest conversation about this subject because it keeps happening to people we know. Adultery is another 800-pound gorilla in the room. If you remember, the first temptation I gave in this list was flirting. I wonder how many times adultery began with eye contact and an "innocent" little flirt. Every time! If for no other reason, we need to wrestle with this temptation for the single purpose of curtailing its frequency. We need to dissect it and analyze it and get honest with it.

How many times have "perfect" Christians thought about adultery? I'll bet you there are more than you'd ever want to imagine. Why do you think I'm writing a book about temptation? It's because there are no perfect Christians. Therefore, an honest conversation confronting the gorillas in the room is exactly the medicine the church needs in our pervasive culture of tolerance, denial and betrayal.

Indeed, adultery is an 800-pound temptation in the room with your name on it. You think it can't happen to you. Wake up and smell the coffee! (P.S.: The grass *is not* greener on the other side of the fence!)

11. Movies.

Feeling defensive already? Let's be honest for a change. R-rated movies do not make us better Christians. There is either swearing or violence or sex or a combination thereof in every R-rated movie made these days.

There are also milder movies that are just as bad for our souls. If it doesn't edify, and if it isn't pure, and if it doesn't follow Philippians 4:8, then probably—just maybe—we shouldn't be watching it. I know this leaves us out of the loop on a lot of cultural relevancy. Sewage plants are relevant, but I don't spend time in them either. I just know they are there.

If your first inclination is to defend what you watch and deem me a misfit, then temptation has done a masterful job on your mind and heart. Temptation is the professor in the classroom of controversy. Temptation is the professor in the arena of cultural tolerance.

I grew up with a song I learned as a little boy. The funny thing of it is that this song is more relevant for me as an adult than what it was for me as a child: "Oh be careful little eyes what you see. Oh be careful little feet where you go. Oh be careful little ears what you hear. Oh be careful little mouth what you say. For the Father up above is looking down in love, so be careful little child what you see." Movies are a temptation that often takes us away from God. And even if it's only for ten seconds, that's too long!

12. Fudging on taxes.

Yikes! You probably didn't think I'd bring this one up. For years, I had a friend, who knew what he was doing, do my taxes. It turned out he was doing one part of them wrong. I got a lovely letter from the IRS. In fact, they were so fond of me and my family they wanted to pay a visit to our home. In fact, they liked me so much they brought a friend just to share the love.

It was like a play being reviewed in the NFL. Upon further review, as it turned out, my friend had made the same mistake on my taxes year after year. Not a big deal; it was only money. Yeah right! It was a big deal! I had to pay back three years worth of mistakes—with interest. It was an awful experience, and I didn't even know I was doing them wrong because I wasn't doing them. It appeared I was cheating on my taxes. I wasn't cheating; they had simply been wrong.

Fudging is when you intentionally pay less than what you owe. Trust me, it isn't worth it. Be honest. Pay what you owe and move on. For some, this is a point of temptation for multiple reasons. It isn't worth it. Don't let the temptation of fudging on your taxes become your temptation of choice.

13. Avoiding gifts to God.

Depending on what survey you go by, only 3% of Christians tithe! When you give less than a tithe, that is called a tip. I'm amazed at how many people want God to help them with finances (and for that matter just about everything else in life), yet they deliberately ignore God's principles on sowing and reaping.

The tithe is simply 10% of my income that I give to God through the local church. Offerings are what I give on top of my tithe. I have always tithed, so for me this one is a yawner. This isn't a book on giving, but if it were I would share overwhelming evidence that supports the tithe.

I've never heard one person who tithes say they regret tithing. Yet, I hear people complain about everything from finances, to their marriages, to their difficult lives, and as to why the sky is about to fall on them. Funny thing, the common thread is a failure to be a generous giver. Giving is an attitude that flows from love and manifests itself in tangible ways. It is God's way of doing business.It is impossible to experience God's blessings in your life if you are ignoring Him with your lack of giving. Give God a chance on this one. Has He ever let you down? My son died at age sixteen, and I can tell you that even in that awful experience, not once has God ever let me down—not once! Ignoring the joys of giving is a temptation you don't want to be guilty of.

Further, we have the high privilege of giving God our time as a valued gift. We seem to lack enough time to do the things we want to do, yet have enough time to do the things we *really* want to do. This morning as I write this paragraph, I am leaving shortly to go to our church to help do some chores before Easter to make the church look a little nicer. (It already looks awesome with all the regular volunteers who keep it looking so nice both inside and out.) I got home last night after driving sixteen hours straight from southern California. I am going because it is a priority, not because I have the time, but because I am *making* the time. I am certain it will be the most gratifying thing I do all day! Those are the kinds of feelings we get when we do something for God. We all have the same amount of time allotted to us. It is our highest privilege to give God our time. We are capable of changing our world, not just with money, but with time, which is the essence of relationships.

14. Lack of Bible reading.

There's always a temptation to do everything in Christianity but read the Bible. It's like running. You never really want to start, but when you're finished you're very glad you went for the run. So it is with reading the Bible; it's usually tough getting started, but once you finish you're always glad you did it.

The temptation is to fill our time with other very legitimate important things. Then when someone asks, "Have you read your Bible today?" we hang our heads and reveal the answer without ever saying a word. Honestly, I've been a Christian for more than 45 years and a pastor for more than 30 years and I still have to work at making time to read my Bible every day. Truthfully, there are days that I miss.

Like I said, we all can be messed up. There really is no such thing as a perfect Christian. Of all the temptations to be a part of, temptation loves it when you don't read your Bible. Food for thought!

15. Gossiping.

It is really fun to talk about other people, right? Gossiping is probably the single greatest temptation in the church. Everyone likes to hear a juicy story, don't they? I have no idea how we're going to tackle this temptation. What I know is it has hurt more people than I can count.

Why do we like to talk about other people's problems so much? If they were our own we wouldn't like to talk about them. Yet, we love getting in on a juicy story. Maybe every church in America should hear a sermon titled, "Keep Your Big Fat Mouth Shut." I honestly believe that sometimes we gossip and don't even think it's gossiping. I don't know what we think we're doing, but we would not classify the conversation as gossip.

Most things that are said simply don't need to be said. Temptation loves to get us on this one. Temptation wants us to talk about someone as though we're doing them a favor when in reality we're doing quite the opposite. Temptation is a crafty one. Gossip is one of temptation's most enjoyable habits. I know some struggle with this one a bunch. If it isn't good, kind, or edifying, then let's leave it alone.

16. Homosexuality.

I realize I've just ticked some people off. But follow this line of reasoning with me if you will. If this behavior was normal, it would be able to sustain life, and it cannot. Therefore, homosexuality is not normal. It is an alternative lifestyle. It is not a normal lifestyle. It's even a temptation for some to bury their heads in the sand and pretend it's a normal lifestyle. It may have become common because people have been coerced by fear into keeping their mouths shut if they think it is not acceptable, but that doesn't mean it is normal.

Common and normal are two entirely different words with very different meanings. Have you ever been to a funeral knowing death was caused by complications from AIDS? I have, and in my opinion that is not normal. It is an extra sad thing; at least, it was for me.

Because of fear, people are silent on the subject if they think it isn't a normal lifestyle. I'm simply saying it's an unhealthy temptation because if it were normal it would be able to sustain itself and it cannot. Homosexuality is an alternative lifestyle that for some is a temptation. Isn't it astounding how temptation can deceive us?

17. Lying.

Here's a temptation for the ages. Everyone has lied—at least in my generation. I have lied and I am sure you have as well. White lies are black lies that have been bleached. You can clean a pig up, put Chanel No. 5 on the pig, but it's still a pig.

Lying is a temptation that touches every arena of life. We lie for lots and lots of reasons, none of which are legitimate. Lying is so acceptable in our culture that I'm afraid the dictionary people are one day going to change its definition. That is exactly what temptation wants us to do by lying—change the perception of the truth.

When you change the meaning, you make the poison more deadly. Changing the label on a bottle of poison to something nonlethal makes the poison more lethal—not less lethal. With a watered-down label you have no idea the harm it can cause.

This is what temptation has done with lying. It has changed the label, and the damage lying causes is far worse now because our culture lives in denial of what lying really is. Temptation has won the battle on this issue in our culture. Avoid letting temptation win this battle in your life. Tell the truth all the time.

18. Greed.

We call this temptation the "American Dream." It turns out we should have named it the "American Nightmare." Because of greed, our economy is all messed up. Because of greed, people have their priorities upside down. Because of greed, people have become selfish and self-centered. Because of greed, families are spending less time together. Because of greed, people are less happy, not happier. Because of greed, there are some who are ruining it for everyone else.

Greed robs us of contentment. Greed takes away our joy. Greed turns us into vicious animals. Greed causes family to turn on family. As a pastor, from time to time I get involved in a family's fight in an effort to resolve the fairness of the distribution of the will after a parent has died. Families do not want what is fair or what their loved one wanted; they want as much as they can get. It is called greed, plain and simple.

The line we cross over to become people of greed must be an invisible line because so many people do it. Temptation has made the line invisible so once we have crossed over the line it's too late to turn back. Temptation is cruel when it comes to greed. For having so much, through the temptation of greed, it's amazing to me how little one actually has!

19. Idolatry.

This is a huge temptation that has many names in our culture, the least of which is called idolatry. Although we probably don't bow down to idols, idolatry is anything that takes the place of God in our lives. So you see, an idol can be just about anything. There are many idols in our culture. They come in different shapes and sizes. Sometimes idolatry looks like time. Other times idolatry looks like a friend. Other times idolatry looks like pleasure. Other times idolatry looks like money. Other times idolatry looks like a game or a sport. Other times idolatry looks like a famous person.

Idolatry has many faces that rarely carry the name "idolatry." Temptation has carefully masked idolatry to not look like idolatry. Temptation has made idolatry look pretty, smell pretty, and talk pretty. It compliments us and becomes so addicting that when it has our heart it's too late to turn back. Temptation is that way when it comes to idolatry.

At the heart of idolatry is the death of God. That is temptation's ultimate goal: to kill God. Temptation is subtle, has lots of time and is very patient when it comes to idols in our lives. Idolatry is a nasty temptation. Recognize the many faces of idolatry and run away from it as fast as you can!

20. Abortion.

The temptation for many pregnant women is to take what appears to be the easy way out. Abortion is never the easy way out. Abortion carries with it scar tissue on several levels. It carries with it memories that will haunt you until the day you die. For the one who has had an abortion: thank God for healing and restoration. For the one reading this book considering an abortion, please do not have an abortion!

It is at this point that temptation really makes me angry. Temptation takes no prisoners and has no friends except for the friends of misery and regret.

Allow me to say something to the men reading this who are taking part in abortions too. You can honor God by encouraging the one you got pregnant to have the baby.

21. Witchcraft.

Horoscopes. Psychics. Are these really necessary in your life? Some consider these amusements of curiosity. Isn't it amazing the number temptation has pulled over on us on this one? Talk about a sucker punch.

Temptation wants you to think these temptations are innocent and meaningless. Don't be deceived by these things. They are satanic worship in disguise. These temptations are just as strong and addictive as many of the other temptations in this chapter.

If you underestimate temptation on this one, temptation will cut your legs off and leave you to bleed to death. Your experience may be that dabbling in these things was perfectly harmless. That's what most alcoholics say about their first sip of alcohol—perfectly harmless! Temptation wants you to underestimate this one big time. Don't be a victim. Leave these things alone.

If you want to know the future, read your Bible and listen to God; He will tell you everything you want to know about the future!

22. Prejudice.

This temptation is as old as time. Prejudice not only of color and race but of social status and intellectual status as well. Prejudice comes in many different sizes and shapes, and they all are ugly—every single one of them. How we got the idea that one person is better than another because of some external factor just goes to show the power behind temptation. It is awful to see in action. On the other hand, it is beautiful to see harmony among people who fail to exercise prejudice.

I would love to see prejudice eradicated during my lifetime. I'm not going to hold my breath for it to happen. Our problem is that we are so cozy with temptation that we tolerate the temptation of prejudice as though it were inevitable. Prejudice can be avoided if the beast of temptation is better identified.

Temptation has one goal: to destroy. So let's deal temptation a blow and start working together. This conversation needs to take us to places where we find reasons to be together and live with one another because of what we have in common rather than live apart because of what we don't have in common. Prejudice is a nasty, awful temptation that we can do better against!

23. Lust.

This temptation is as big as they come. There are many things for which someone can lust. The most common one is sexual, so let's go with that one. I was taught something by my aunt when I was in junior high in a Sunday school class. I have no idea why I remember her lesson that day because I had no idea what she was talking about as far as the subject matter went. I think she was talking about the birds and the bees. I grew up so sheltered that I thought she was talking about the birds and the bees. I'm guessing she was talking about boys and girls and the stuff they can do with one another, especially when they don't have any clothes on.

I was bored that morning. However, she gave a little lesson God burned in my brain, not for that day but for many other days to come in my life, including this day. She gave us the four Ls: Look, Long, Linger, Lust. That was it. She said when you look long enough you will start to long for that which you look at. And when you have looked at something long enough, you will linger over that which you do not have. And when you have lingered over someone in a way that requires the first three Ls, you'll complete the cycle and lust. I've never forgotten that.

Temptation does not want you to know about the four Ls. That's why I gave them to you—so you will be without excuse. You now know how lust becomes a viable temptation. By the way, if you glance, it is not lust. If you take a second look with intent, it is lust! Stay away from this temptation; it's a killer!

24. Pride.

One of the meanest of all the temptations is pride. This temptation will make all the other temptations I have listed look like child's play. This temptation will destroy families faster than a blazing fire. This storm is a category 5, and there is nowhere to hide. Stay away from this one at all costs; otherwise it will cost you everything you have.

The temptation to exercise pride is very powerful. It has destroyed everything from friendships to families to churches to nations to where people will spend eternity. I urge you to live a life of humility and do everything you can to stay away from this monster.

Temptation wants you to crave this beast. It cannot be tamed or controlled. It must never be picked up. When picked up, you can't get it off your hands. The stains of pride go into the blood. May God help all of us to run away from the temptation of pride.

These have been 24 of the major temptations we face. The list isn't exhaustive—there are really as many as the sands of the shore. I simply wanted to get some temptations down on paper so the conversation can take place. The goal is to tackle and tame temptation. It begins with a thoughtful conversation, using some very specific subjects. I have tried to create the topics. It's up to you and your friends to create the resolve to conquer temptation.

Temptation does not want you to know what it gives birth to, so I will tell you. Temptation, when yielded to, becomes sin. Sin is the child of temptation. It is a child that is born grown-up and mean and evil. It is a child that is worse than its parent, temptation. It is a child that is not a child at all. It is the monster of monsters. It is the enemy of enemies.

But thank God, He has given us a weapon that can kill sin: the precious blood of Jesus Christ. Sin is big, but the blood of Jesus Christ is bigger. What sin does to destroy, the blood of Jesus Christ does to heal and far more. The blood of Jesus Christ will never ever lose its power. It reaches to wherever you are. The blood of Christ will give you and me strength each and every day to face temptation and win.

I once wrote a lesson in 1985 entitled, "How to Face Temptation and Win." The answer is in the blood of Jesus Christ. So you see, temptation in life is great, but the blood of Jesus Christ is far greater!

SCRIPTURES ON DELIVERANCE

1. The LORD is my rock, my fortress, and my deliverer (2 Samuel 22:2).
2. If you keep silent at this time, liberation and deliverance will come to the Jewish people from another place, but you and your father's house will be destroyed. Who knows, perhaps you have come to the kingdom for such a time as this (Esther 4:14).
3. The LORD is my rock, my fortress, and my deliverer, my God, my mountain where I seek refuge, my shield and the horn of my salvation, my stronghold (Psalm 18:2).
4. He relies on the LORD; let Him rescue him; let the LORD deliver him, since He takes pleasure in him (Psalm 22:8).

5. The Spirit of the Lord is on Me, because He has anointed Me to preach good news to the poor. He has sent Me to proclaim freedom to the captives and recovery of sight to the blind, to set free the oppressed, to proclaim the year of the Lord's favor (Luke 4:18–19).
6. And forgive us our sins, for we ourselves also forgive everyone in debt to us. And do not bring us into temptation (Luke 11:4).
7. He assumed his brothers would understand that God would give them deliverance through him, but they did not understand (Acts 7:25).
8. He has delivered us from such a terrible death, and He will deliver us; we have placed our hope in Him that He will deliver us again (2 Corinthians 1:10).
9. Who gave Himself for our sins to rescue us from this present evil age, according to the will of our God and Father, to whom be the glory forever and ever. Amen (Galatians 1:4–5).
10. And free those who were held in slavery all their lives by the fear of death (Hebrews 2:15).

LESSON #6

1. Genesis 3:1–13. How were Adam and Eve delivered? Why or why not?
2. Genesis 39:1–23. How was Joseph delivered? Why?
3. Job 1:1–22. How was Job delivered? Why?
4. Matthew 4:1–11. How was Jesus delivered? Why?
5. 1 John 2:1–6. How are we delivered? Why or why not?
6. Psalm 139:1–24. Read the entire passage.
    a. Who is the best forecaster? (God). Discuss.
    b. What is our best help? (Scripture). Discuss.
    c. Who will bring us deliverance? (Holy Spirit). Discuss.
    d. Who else can help me? (accountability partner). Discuss.
    e. How can I help myself? (Create a simple plan). Discuss, develop.

7. Helps…
   a. How much time have you spent with the Holy Spirit today?
   b. Have you prayed enough today?
   c. Have you spent enough time in the Bible today?
   d. Have you taken a walk today with Jesus?

CHAPTER 7

DIVERTING TEMPTATION

So far, I've attempted to lay out temptation in a fairly thorough manner. At last, it's time to delve into some solutions to temptation.

I don't think there is a way to eliminate temptation as much as there are ways to divert it, so that's where our focus is for this chapter. I'll give you 18 ways, minus 1, for you to create a diversion against temptation. You have probably noticed that I have given temptation a life of its own in this book. That's because temptation is alive and well. I know temptation is not a person, but for not being a person, it seems to have plenty of lives.

None of these tactics are meant to be used alone. I'm going to an El Salvadorian restaurant for lunch today with my daughter Kristi. I have no intention of ordering just one item off the menu. I will start with chips and salsa. Then I'll order something that includes beans and rice. I usually get the special of the day. But I order my food in combination. I eat it the same way. I know some people eat one item at a time on their plate until it is gone, then they tackle another item on the plate. Not me. Whatever food is on my plate had better look out because it's not long for this world. The only thing safe when I am eating is the plate!

These diversions are meant to be used in combination with one another. And sometimes the combinations will change based on the situation. I urge you to find a combination that works for you. Be flexible and willing to change it up if necessary. Have a conversation with others about which of these diversions work best for you in combination. Remember, we need to help one another fight temptation.

18 ANSWERS MINUS 1

1. *Discipline.*

I know this isn't a very attractive word to a lot of people, but it's a necessary one in the war against temptation. For those who are not fond of this word, it's not as bad as it appears. I hope to give you a perspective that will make it easier to swallow so you don't gag on the idea.

Discipline is a huge weapon against temptation. If we're going to push back against our formidable foe, then discipline has to be on the front lines of the battle. In a hurricane, the cellar is a lifesaver. In the storms of life where temptation is causing hell, discipline becomes the cellar that brings protection and safety and security. It is essential.

I like to play golf. By the rules of the game, a golfer is allowed to have 14 clubs in the bag. Every golfer has their favorite club. For me it's my sand wedge. I love that club because I do better with it than with any other club in the bag. I use it on almost every hole because all my other shots are so lousy these days. I rarely hit a green in regulation, which means my sand wedge gets a lot of playing time. It is the one club that gets me closest to the hole so my putter can do the rest.

I remember a round of golf I played several years ago because I hadn't played in 5 years. (It's a long story why I had not played; suffice it to say I had more rust in my game than a bucket of nails resting on the ocean floor for the past century.) I hit my first tee shot into the water and it never got better from there. However, on the fourth hole, after hacking it down the fairway, I hit my fourth shot into the hole from about 60 yards out. I used my trusty sand wedge. In fact, on another hole I chipped in with my sand wedge.

Discipline is the one club in our bag that can help us get closest to the hole. Temptation represents all the out-of-bounds stakes on a golf course. It represents all of the hazard stakes on the golf course. All of us need that one club in the bag that can help us recover from a bad shot. Temptation is that bad shot. Discipline is that club in the bag that helps us recover from the hazards of temptations!

2. *A Plan.*

A plan never hurts—and it always helps. Many times temptation gets the best of us because we fail to have a plan. As the saying goes, "If you fail to plan, you can plan to fail." This is so true in life. Planning really is the partner of discipline. When you exercise discipline in your life, it means you have a plan for your life.

I challenge you to develop a plan so you can conquer temptation in your life. This will be truly liberating for you. You'll feel like you're at the top of your game if you develop a practical plan to help you fight temptation. If your plan is not practical it's not a plan that's worth having. It needs to work. Be willing to adjust the plan to the situation, but have a plan!

Plans require several things in order to make a positive difference. Your plan requires thinking time. Your plan requires a review of the times your enemy, temptation, has won the battle in your life. You need to have a good dose of honesty. You need to be willing to change some of your habits and patterns in your daily routine.

I have lots of friends who are cops. Working as a chaplain for the police department puts me in a circle of cops that I enjoy very much. One of my cop friends rarely takes the same road to a routine destination. He's always mixing it up because as a detective he's made several enemies over the years. Therefore, he changes his daily routine in order to ensure a higher level of safety for him and his family. This is what I mean by having a plan that works.

Assuming temptation is the enemy, we need to have a plan that will catch temptation off guard. If temptation knows our routine, then it will be able to more easily trip us up. But, if temptation doesn't know our next move then temptation won't be able to snare us as easily. See what I'm talking about?

A plan is crucial in diverting temptation. Keep in mind that we're talking about diverting temptation, not ending temptation. As I've said in other places, temptation is here to stay. But with careful planning we can keep temptation on the run. Think of it as a game if you will. Temptation needs to become the loser in our lives. With a plan couched in discipline we'll begin winning the battle against temptation.

Think of planning as your favorite club in the bag. So temptation has gotten the best of you and you're living your life right now on the wrong side of the out-of-bound markers in life. Develop a plan and start swinging away at temptation!

3. *Help from others.*

Everyone needs somebody once in a while. If the truth be known, we need each other more than we ever would want to admit. Without endorsing or bashing Hillary Clinton, I've read her book on the village and the individual, and she makes a good point. We are connected to and with one another. Yet, I think we think that when it comes to temptation, it's every man for himself.

The intent of this book is to create an environment where a conversation can take place on a subject that has been taboo for a long time so we can better deliver a knock-out blow to our enemy: temptation.

Temptation is a formidable opponent. I think of the times I've surfed through the channels only to land on the one where there is wrestling. I'm not sure why they call it wrestling because it doesn't look like wrestling to me. It is a cross between a circus and a group date gone wrong. In any event, it seems like in those situations everyone is fighting everyone else. I'm not sure anyone knows why they are hitting (fake-hitting, I might add) each other. Who is the enemy? Who is the opponent? This is how it seems with temptation. (For you wrestling fans, please avoid the temptation to hate me or correct me!)

We're all in the ring of life and we too look like a cross between a circus and a group date gone wrong. We're hitting and hurting one another. Unlike wrestling on television, our swings are landing direct blows and we're hurting one another. We need to call a time-out and reflect on why we're hitting one another. The enemy is temptation, not each other. Temptation started the brawl, and like the yellow-livered coward it is, temptation has slithered out of the ring only to sit in the front row to watch the festivities.

Imagine what would happen if we directed our efforts toward temptation as a group. This is the conversation I'm inviting you to have with one another.

4. *Accountability.*

This is different from helping one another, although it is a form of doing so. It's a much more targeted and specific club in the bag. It involves one-on-one care. If you have this sort of a person in your life, someone who is keeping you on the straight and narrow, then consider yourself blessed.

Of course, you need to find a way to do this that really works for you. I've never been very good at being part of an accountability group. I have many friends who are part of such a group and they swear by them. I tried to be part of such a group years ago. There were three of us who were friends and we thought we'd start an accountability group together. So we met the first time in my office. It was a disaster. Nobody wanted to go first and nobody wanted to share. Any other time we would laugh and talk and joke and goof off together. But place us in a room under the caption "accountability" and we became three blind (make that mute) mice. At our second meeting a week later, we at least talked to one another. At that meeting we decided not to meet again!

My accountability partner is my wife. You need to find someone in your life you can be brutally honest with. For me, that is my wife. And one of the rules of accountability is you have to be willing to hear things that might (and probably will) make you mad. This is the nature of accountability. We have to sit there and take the honest evaluations others give.

I want to give to you two points of caution about using accountability as a means to divert temptation. The first is that after you're finished with your accountability partner, you still have time to go into a dark room and listen to temptation. An accountability partner is only a help, not the final answer.

The second point is that accountability only works if you're honest. I have the privilege of seeing many people arrested during my time with cops. I'm amazed at how many times people lie through their teeth. (Of course, the ones on meth don't have many teeth to lie through!)

If accountability is going to work in diverting temptation, you have to tell the truth all of the time without conveniently leaving out parts of the story.

So, who is your accountability partner?

5. *A back-up plan.*

This is my favorite point in this entire chapter. I love back-up plans because the original plan rarely works the way it was intended! Back-up plans show vision and discernment.

Because our enemy temptation is so elusive and cunning and underhanded, we would be crazy not to have a back-up plan. A back-up plan is nothing more than forecasting what is likely to happen if the first plan doesn't meet the need. In fact, I have discovered the back-up plan more times than not is more important than the first plan.

Whenever I am in an intense round of negotiations with my wife, I have "Plan A," and I always have "Plan B" ready to go. One of the situations where I use a back-up plan more often than not is when I try to figure out which restaurant my wife wants to go to for dinner. As I am writing this draft, I think we're going out for dinner tonight. I have a first choice where I think she'll want to go. Just in case I am wrong (and I usually am on this one), I have a second choice to present to her. Of course, if neither of those works then the third option is a toasted cheese sandwich at home tonight! (If it were up to me the toasted cheese sandwich would be my first choice.)

I've been married for more than 30 years, and back-up plans are the backbone of my marriage. Now let's apply planning and back-up planning to temptation. I do not believe it's optional to forgo a back-up plan. Be creative and be smart in your deliberations.

If you have a problem with pornography and you're tempted every time you go by a porn shop on your way to work, your first plan might be to take a different route. Your back-up plan might be to be on the phone with your accountability partner every time you are about to drive by the shop. Pretty radical stuff, but then again, temptation is a pretty radical monster!

6. *God's divine intervention.*

This diversion is by far the most powerful of all the items I list in this chapter. Nothing can take the place of God's divine intervention. In fact, if we could count on this one, we would have no need of the others.

I have often wondered why God doesn't make things easier for us. I've often wondered why He's not more involved in helping us out. The truth of the matter is that God does help us out. But He's interested in more than just confronting and diverting temptation. It is apparent God is working on a specimen called character. He also cares a great deal about faith. He also seems to give attention to prayer.

There are lots of things that God considers when you and I might think divine intervention should happen. Perhaps a better way of stating it would be that God usually intervenes indirectly. I'm looking for more direct divine intervention. It would make my battle with temptation a whole lot easier. But then, let's consider what that might look like with a specific temptation.

Take the temptation of lust. Let's suppose I look at a girl who is naked. Indirect divine intervention might be the Holy Spirit speaking to my heart, telling me that is wrong. That happens to me all the time with temptation—not that I am looking at naked girls, but that the Holy Spirit speaks to my heart. Divine intervention could include blindness for twenty-four hours! That would be divine intervention I would not want. Can you imagine explaining that one to your wife? Can you imagine explaining that one to your boss?

I'm glad God does it just the way He does it because that kind of direct divine intervention would be shameful. On the other hand, it might become a great deterrent. Give this some thought in your conversation with one another. You might come up with some really interesting ways God could show His divine intervention to us.

7. Scripture.

This is the second best way I know to divert temptation. I've laced this book with Scriptures that I hope will help and encourage you. There are many ways to utilize the Scriptures. You can read the Scriptures in mass volume and they will help to divert temptation. You can read the Scriptures for deep study and that will definitely divert temptation, especially if you topically attack the landmines that protect temptation.

You can memorize the Scriptures, which will help divert temptation too. However, in my life I've found that when I'm confronted with temptation, I don't immediately think of verses that I can use as scud missiles. More often than not, I find myself shooting blanks at temptation when I'm in the heat of battle.

I think the general rule of thumb is that the more time you spend in the Scriptures the less time you'll spend with temptation. The general idea is to spend lots of time in the Scriptures. A great conversation to have with others would be to define what it means to have "lots of time in the Scriptures."

I would encourage you to err on the side of more, not less. In fact, if temptation still has the upper hand in our lives, then we need to spend even more time in the Scriptures. Remember, this diversion doesn't stand alone. In fact, none of these are meant to stand alone. They are to be used in combination with other tactics.

8. Eternal perspective.

I know I've already beaten this drum elsewhere, but this diversion is so important I must mention it one more time. We all have an eternal perspective. Usually it is kept in the corner of our brain behind some other things that are no longer important to us. We're glad for eternity and an eternal perspective, just not now. That eternity stuff is for later when I need it. Wrong! We need it now for lots of reasons.

On January 6, 2003, I came home from work to find my son Kevin unconscious upstairs. After I performed pathetic CPR on him, he was taken by ambulance to the hospital where he never regained consciousness. One hundred hours later, he was in heaven. This kind of event forces you to go into the attic of your brain and pull out eternity. Inside eternity you find an eternal perspective.

I now live my life with an eternal perspective in mind. It changes everything. It doesn't take the death of a child to have an eternal perspective. You can learn from others on this one. (If you want to know the whole story of my son and what I learned from that tragedy, it is the foundation for my first book, *Reclaiming Heaven's Covenant.)*

My point is that if you have an eternal perspective you'll approach temptation much differently than if you don't have an eternal perspective. If you're thinking eternally, you will spend so much less time entertaining temptation, because there are other things far more important to spend your time on.

The conversation I invite you to have with others on this diversion is to find ways to strip away the "stuff" in life that keeps us living for the moment. Find ways to think about tomorrow so you can have a better today so your yesterdays will not be filled with sad memories.

9. *Inner person development.*

What in heaven's name is this one? This one is all about character. Then why wouldn't I just say character? Because these three words—*inner person development*—put together are very powerful.

What happens to our outside with temptation happens because of what first has happened on the inside. This battle with temptation is against our person. And life is more than a journey. It is a process where we develop, not evolve. We never reach a level of perfection in this life, but we can reach levels of manageability with things like temptation. This diversion is the culmination of all the others put together. It comes about when we sit down at the table and lay out all the pieces to the puzzle. Inner person development comes as we put together those pieces. Although we will never arrive at perfection, we can have a level of development that will make life better.

The goal of inner person development is to make life better as we combat our enemy. This diversion to temptation comes in bits and pieces, but it comes nonetheless. It comes with age and maturity. It comes as a direct result of intentionally working at life instead of living a life of defeat with an "it doesn't matter" attitude. This is a great one to have a conversation about because others can help us see ourselves in a light we may not consider. You can be an encouragement to others as they are an encouragement to you. Together in conversation, we can spur one another on to further inner person development. In one regard it takes a village. In another regard, we are on our own. Whether we are together or alone, temptation still comes knocking at our door.

10. Big picture.

Seeing the entire lay of the land allows us to see beyond the immediate temptation we are battling.

I don't like flying very much. Maybe it all started when my roommate in college, who had just gotten his pilot's license, took me up for a short spin. I should have seen the warning signs when he pulled the plane out from where it was parked. Yikes!

We took off, and I should have seen another warning sign when he said to "hang on" and then started laughing like a monster in a movie. Milliseconds later he dropped the tail of the plane and we were free-falling. (I now know what one small part of hell is like.) He then said to "hang on" once again and he was right. He pointed the plane straight downward (at least that's what it felt like) and I thought I was going to die. But as much as I hate flying, the view from above always reminds me that you get an entirely different picture of life when you can look down and see the big picture than you do when you're stuck on the ground, going through sometimes scary and confusing things. The big picture of life allows you to see temptation for what it is and put it into perspective against the rest of life. This allows us to expose temptation, thereby diverting it away from our lives.

11. Convictions.

If we have biblical convictions, they will affect how we approach temptation. If we don't have biblical convictions, our approach to temptation will be weakened, we will be weakened, and temptation will become a powerful foe.

Convictions are those nonnegotiables in our lives that do not change with time or culture. A conviction is one of the strongest emotions, based on reason and study, that we can have in this life. Convictions are a game-changer. We're each in need of a set of convictions that can tell temptation to take a hike! Convictions are the roots of our souls. They go as deep as anything else we possess. They aren't swayed by popular opinion. They aren't open to a bribe. They are the foundation of civilization. They are the fountain from which flows the clean pure water.

Temptation seeks to devour convictions. Temptation seeks to destroy the roots of convictions. Temptation is the enemy of biblical convictions. In our conversations with others, it is helpful for us to articulate our convictions. Discover how deep the roots of conviction go in your soul. Have others challenge you with scenarios that would sever your convictions all for the sake of a fleeting temptation. This is where iron can sharpen iron. This is the lab room for our souls. This is where we test and formulate convictions that will divert temptations in our lives.

12. Biblical worldview.

If we don't have a biblical worldview, we will get pulverized by temptation. I teach this subject at a local university. I love it because many think they have a biblical worldview when in realty it is only a partial biblical worldview.

All temptation needs is a small opening to undress us in public. Temptation will tell us we have on the finest of clothes and that people are staring because we look so beautiful. The reality is that temptation has undressed us and we don't even realize it. People are staring, not because we are beautiful, but because we are buck naked! That is the result of a partial biblical worldview.

I teach that in the United States anything short of a biblical worldview leads to moral socialism. Socialism is temptation's friend because the standard has been set so low that individual responsibility has been stripped away until there is no longer any personal accountability left. Temptation loves socialism. Lessen the view of the Bible and you lessen the view of God. Lessen the view of God and you empower temptation.

In your conversation with others I invite you to discuss the truth or falsehood of what I am saying. Temptation has a throne because God has been taken off the throne. God has been taken off the throne because the Bible has been devalued in our culture. It hasn't always been like that. It's the way it is now. This is why temptation is running wild. It is a cancer that has seemingly no cure. By the way we live and act, it has the appearance of being unstoppable. But a true biblical worldview can stop it in its tracks.

13. A fear of hell.

Yep, you heard me right. The goal is to find a way to divert away from temptation. When you run temptation all the way out to its final chapter, you end up in hell.

I have had a fear of hell since I was a little boy. I got saved while listening to a sermon on hell. I'm currently researching another book I plan to write on the theology of hell. I've had a healthy respect for hell my entire life. It has not lessened; it has increased. It helps to keep me on the straight and narrow. If you believe in universalism, then you don't believe this point is valid because you ultimately believe there is no hell. I think universalism is one of the biggest frauds ever invented. If there is no hell, then there is no temptation. The reason temptation is such a big deal is that it has consequences. If there are no consequences, then temptation is a moot subject. The evidence that there are consequences to temptation gives evidence to the reality of hell and the falsehood of universalism.

In your conversation with one another, consider the consequences of temptation. Consider where temptations come from and why they are game-changers. Try to see the connection between the consequences of temptation and the reality of a real place called hell. A fear of hell will help create a diversion away from temptation. It really works for me; it might work for you!

14. A covenant relationship with God.

The first book I had published is about how to gain a covenant relationship with God and then have it spread into every other relationship in your life. I discovered this covenant relationship with God after my son Kevin went to heaven. That relationship had always been there; I just had never experienced it as deeply.

This single emphasis alone will change how you deal with temptation. It has changed how I approach the beast. If you know that God wants to be with you more than anything else in the world, then you begin to realize He really is a God of love.

When you realize Christianity is not a religion but a relationship, you realize He really wants to spend time with you. When you recognize Christianity is not a list of rules and do's and don'ts, you begin to understand God wants to have something very special with you this side of heaven.

When your motivation for being a Christian is love, everything changes. I have learned that when you try to be a perfect Christian, love is not part of the deal. It's all about rules and crossing the t's and dotting the i's. And then—just maybe—if all the planets are lined up just right, you can have a day of Christian perfection.

I got tired of trying to be perfect. Now I am loved. It's far better than trying to be perfect. I spent years trying to give God all of me. In a covenant relationship with Him, I discovered the roles are reversed. Now I am experiencing all of God, or at least more than I have ever known before.

A covenant relationship is not a contract; it is a covenant. Everything you have and do and are is birthed out of a loving relationship with a loving God. It's worth experiencing.

When it comes to covenant, I'm thinking more about God than I am the temporary satisfaction temptation can offer. I am motivated by love. While love has no boundaries, it has the very best of boundaries.

The way I now live and act isn't because there are rules hanging over my head but because love is in my heart. In covenant, you experience the very best God has to offer. Here's the deal: When you experience this relationship with God, you don't want to go to bed with temptation. In fact, you want to evict temptation from your home and your heart.

In covenant, you experience the very best God has to offer. Here's the deal: When you experience this relationship with God, you don't want to go to bed with temptation. In fact, you want to evict temptation from your home and your heart.

A covenant relationship with God is far more powerful than all the temptations put together. I invite you to spend time with friends figuring out if you have room for more of God in your life. If you don't have room for more of God, it's probably because you have too much temptation living in your life. Temptation wants all of you. God wants all of you. When you come to the place that you want all of God, then you will lose interest in having all of temptation. You will discover a covenant relationship with God is the best remedy for overcoming addictions. A covenant relationship with God is the greatest addiction in all of life! Covenant is more than a diversion from temptation; it is a game-changer!

15. The mind of Christ.

This one is huge! If you have the mind of Christ, you will be able to handle temptation the way Jesus handled temptation. In the following chapter, Jesus is one of three people I use as a study for properly handling temptation.

Having the mind of Christ is a great way to divert temptation. It allows us to think the way Jesus thinks. How does one think the way Jesus thinks? The best way I know to find out is to read the Gospels (Matthew, Mark, Luke, and John) over and over and note the things Jesus shows us and tells us in them. There are 731 of these statements/actions in the Gospels. The more time you spend in these verses the more of the mind of Christ will develop in you.

Remember what I said about taking some of these diversions in combination? This would be a good one to join together with inner person development (point #9). You can better divert temptation if you have the mind of Christ.

16. Indwelling Holy Spirit.

My goal is not to get theological in this book. But I will share something about this diversion that I hope we all can agree on. The Holy Spirit is a person. He is the one who works in our lives as we are faced with temptation. When we defeat temptation, it is the Holy Spirit doing all the work behind the scenes. Pretty cool stuff as far as I am concerned.

I pity the one who settles for manifestations above a full indwelling of the Holy Spirit. I feel bad for people who ignore the Holy Spirit because they think something weird is going to happen. The indwelling of the Holy Spirit has everything to do with relationship. If the Holy Spirit has control of your car, He will steer you away from temptation. FYI: The Holy Spirit never steers us toward temptation!

I understand my relationship with the Holy Spirit best by using the example of the airplane. He is not the co-pilot. And He is not a backseat driver. He is the pilot. When we understand life best is when our hands are off the steering wheel, allowing God to be God in our lives. This is a tough lesson to learn in life, but one worth pursuing no matter what. It's more along the lines of having the mind of Christ. It's more along the lines of a covenant relationship with God. It's about relationship. You either have an intimate relationship with the Holy Spirit or you have an intimate relationship with temptation. You absolutely cannot have it both ways.

In your conversation I invite you to discover and uncover ways the Holy Spirit can take over the control of your life. You'll find this is a huge diversionary tool that will bring great defeat to your enemy, temptation. You'll have also noticed by now that each of the eight lessons makes mention of the Holy Spirit too. I am big on the Holy Spirit!

17. An awareness of reputation.

This is huge for me. I hope it's huge for all of us. If we don't care about our reputations today, there's a good chance we will care about them one day. We each have one reputation. It is really important how we spend it. I would challenge you to ask others during your time of conversation to share their perception of your reputation. Keep in mind: we can hide a lot of junk from our friends and family. However, it's a great exercise to consider your reputation and how you are perceived as handling temptation.

People may see us as really strong. If they do that's great. It means we're dealing with temptation on a level that's a good example to others. If people see us as otherwise, then it can be a challenge to us to handle temptation better so the perception of our reputation will be an accurate reflection of what is really going on.

I try to use awareness of my reputation as a diversion to temptation all the time because I have a family, as well as children, youth, college students and an entire congregation for whom my reputation matters. Even if there weren't anybody at all watching, I want to be true to myself and to my God. Those are the two biggest motivations in my life. My reputation is a great diversion away from temptation.

18. Disneyland.

That's right. Disneyland! We've all heard it said that Disneyland is the happiest place on earth. Therefore, the way I see it, there probably is not any temptation anywhere near Disneyland. Wrong!

I've been to Disneyland a thousand times or so. It used to be the place we took vacations. We sometimes went to the park more than once in a year. We always bought the annual passes and stayed for seven days or more.

I have a hundred stories I could tell you, but I will limit it to just one for the sake of time. Our family always loved the fireworks show at 9 each evening. Kevin always looked for the best place to watch the show. Our last year there before Kevin went to heaven, he found a place few people had ever thought of to watch the show.

I'm telling you Kevin checked out every possible location in the park. On the last time we were there together, he found what I consider the best place in the park to watch the show. When I tell you the secret, it will be out and probably ruin the spot for the very few who go there. This spot is best when the temperature reaches 90°. This way the pavement warms up. This matters because watching the show from our secret spot requires lying down on your back!

This secret spot is right in front of "It's a Small World." To be more specific, there is a gazebo in front of the ride about 40 yards from the entrance. Just to the left of the gazebo on a warm night when the pavement feels like an electric blanket, lie down and let the show begin. The fireworks explode directly over you where you are. The boom, the smell of sulfur, and the closeness to the fireworks are awesome! For our family it was a slice of heaven on earth.

Tragically, temptation was lying beside us watching the show. During that day, we saw temptations of all sorts, including bad language, bad behavior, and bad attitudes. Not even in Disneyland can you get away from temptation. Disneyland is not a diversion from temptation. This is an important point because we think we can go places on planet earth where temptation is not. Sorry to be the bearer of bad news: Temptation has infected every square inch of the planet. It's important to know you can't run from temptation or hide from it. That is why this chapter is important; we learn how to divert ourselves away from temptation. (Thus, 18 minus 1.)

With others, conclude the conversation on this chapter by talking about the ways that work best for you in diverting temptation and the ways that are the least effective. My thoughts are not exhaustive. Rather, they're meant to be tabletop discussion starters to point you in a direction away from temptation.

Scriptures on Strength

1. Love the Lord your God with all your heart, with all your soul, and with all your strength (Deuteronomy 6:5).
2. The Lord is my strength and my shield; my heart trusts in Him,

and I am helped. Therefore my heart rejoices, and I praise Him with my song (Psalm 28:7).

3. God is our refuge and strength, a helper who is always found in times of trouble (Psalm 46:1).
4. But those who trust in the Lord will renew their strength; they will soar on wings like eagles; they will run and not grow weary; they will walk and not faint (Isaiah 40:31).
5. So he answered me, "This is the word of the LORD to Zerubbabel: 'Not by strength or by might, but by My Spirit,' says the Lord of Hosts" (Zechariah 4:6).
6. But I have prayed for you that your faith may not fail. And you, when you have turned back, strengthen your brothers (Luke 22:32).
7. Finally, be strengthened by the Lord and by His vast strength (Ephesians 6:10).
8. I am able to do all things through Him who strengthens me (Philippians 4:13).
9. I give thanks to Christ Jesus our Lord, who has strengthened me, because He considered me faithful, appointing me to the ministry (1 Timothy 1:12).
10. Therefore strengthen your tired hands and weakened knees, and make straight paths for your feet, so that what is lame may not be dislocated, but healed instead (Hebrews 12:12–13).

LESSON #7

1. Genesis 3:1–13. What could have been Eve's strength?
2. Genesis 39:1–23. What strengths did Joseph have going for him going into the den of temptation?
3. Job 1:1–22. What made Job so strong?
4. Matthew 4:1–11. What advantages did Jesus have?
5. 1 John 2:1–6. What strengths do we possess as Christians?
6. Further on the subject of strengths…
   a. Identify your five greatest spiritual strengths.
   b. Identify your single greatest spiritual strength.

- c. Identify the spiritual strength you most want to possess in the future.
- d. How have you developed your spiritual strengths?
- e. How can you help other Christians develop strengths they may not possess?
- f. Who is a spiritual giant in your life and why?

7. Helps…
   - a. Have you observed the Holy Spirit working in your life today?
   - b. Has prayer made a difference in your life today?
   - c. Did Jesus show up today in your world?
   - d. Did Scripture give you strength for today?

CHAPTER 8

JOSEPH, JOB AND JESUS

There are not a lot of examples in Scripture of people who did really well with temptation on a consistent basis. There are only three that come to mind quickly. I think of Joseph, especially when he was in Potiphar's house. I think of Job, especially what is said about him in the very first verse of the book named after him. It really sets the stage for the entire book. And then, of course, I think of Jesus, who really had a lot of temptations walking around for about three years with a bunch of knuckleheads and religious leaders who were real pieces of work.

The passage that specifically addresses the temptations Jesus faced is found in Matthew 4:1–11. I invite you to join me and then join one another in a conversation about these three people and how they mastered temptation. Discuss how we can model our lives after theirs. They each have something to offer us. Then, think of others in Scripture who did well and identify others who did not do so well with temptation. You'll find this chapter and your discussion helpful with the war on temptation.

JOSEPH – GENESIS 39:1–23

One of my favorite sections in the Bible is Genesis 37–50. I love the life of Joseph. He was young, and God used him. He got mistreated and never became bitter. He was a leader's leader. He loved family more than anything else in the world, including the immense power and fame he acquired later in life. He demonstrated the kind of love and forgiveness Jesus demonstrated on the cross. He was loyal to every relationship he had. He never once turned his back on God but rather sought God in everything he did.

Joseph helped an entire world and never became corrupt in the process. He was able to see visions from God and know what those visions meant. He was a man who never lacked wisdom from God. He seems to be just about as perfect as a human being can be.

Joseph was a brilliant politician. Joseph was a statesman. He never forgot who he was and where he came from. He was truly a man of God. There is one particular chapter though that grabs my attention when addressing this issue of temptation. In Genesis 39:1–23, Joseph faced a temptation that is very common, as is borne out in the results of the survey in the last chapter.

Genesis 39:1–23 reads as follows in the Holman Christian Standard Bible:

> [1] Now Joseph had been taken to Egypt. An Egyptian [named] Potiphar, an officer of Pharaoh and the captain of the guard, bought him from the Ishmaelites who had brought him there.
> [2] The LORD was with Joseph, and he became a successful man, serving in the household of his Egyptian master.
> [3] When his master saw that the LORD was with him and that the LORD made everything he did successful, [4] Joseph found favor in his master's sight and became his personal attendant. Potiphar also put him in charge of his household and placed all that he owned under his authority.
> [5] From the time that he put him in charge of his household and of all that he owned, the LORD blessed the Egyptian's house because of Joseph. The LORD's blessing was on all that he owned, in his house and in his fields. [6] He left all that he owned under Joseph's authority; he did not concern himself with anything except the food he ate.
> Now Joseph was well-built and handsome. [7] After some time his master's wife looked longingly at Joseph and said, "Sleep with me."

8 But he refused and said to his master's wife, "Look, my
master does not concern himself with anything in his
house, and he has put all that he owns under my authority.
9 No one in this house is greater than I am. He has
withheld nothing from me except you, because you are his
wife. So how could I do such a great evil and sin against
God?"

10 Although she spoke to Joseph day after day, he refused to
go to bed with her. 11 Now one day he went into the house
to do his work, and none of the household servants was
there. 12 She grabbed him by his garment and said, "Sleep
with me!" But leaving his garment in her hand, he escaped
and ran outside. 13 When she realized that he had left his
garment with her and had run outside, 14 she called the
household servants. "Look," she said to them, "my husband
brought a Hebrew man to us to make fun of us. He came to
me so he could sleep with me, and I screamed as loud as I
could. 15 When he heard me screaming for help, he left his
garment with me and ran outside."

16 She put Joseph's garment beside her until his master came
home. 17 Then she told him the same story: "The Hebrew
slave you brought to us came to me to make fun of me, 18
but when I screamed for help, he left his garment with me
and ran outside."

19 When his master heard the story his wife told him—
"These are the things your slave did to me"—he was furious
20 and had him thrown into prison, where the king's
prisoners were confined. So Joseph was there in prison.

21 But the LORD was with Joseph and extended kindness to
him. He granted him favor in the eyes of the prison warden.
22 The warden put all the prisoners who were in the prison
under Joseph's authority, and he was responsible for
everything that was done there. 23 The warden did not
bother with anything under Joseph's authority, because the

> LORD was with him, and the LORD made everything that he did successful.

This is an awesome passage of Scripture because temptation like this is still happening today, every day! It is a great passage because we can do what Joseph did. He did not pull off the impossible; he did something that every one of us is capable of doing with the power of God working in our lives.

I like to break passages down verse by verse so we can glean the very most from the passage. When I am done with this I invite you to have a conversation with others so you can covenant together to copy Joseph's response to temptation. This is one time it is ok to be a copycat!

Notice that in verse 2 it says, "The LORD was with Joseph." When we're facing temptation, we need to constantly be reminded that we are not facing it alone. In fact, it's quite the opposite. God is constantly with us. It's a crying shame we do not make better use of God when we're doing battle with temptation. The bottom line is that God is with us in moments of temptation—and all the other times too.

Success follows obedience. The Lord was with Joseph because that is how Joseph wanted it. You can have the same thing as Joseph, and success will be your consequence.

Likewise, verse 2 shows us the consequences of what happens when the Lord is with us and we reciprocate that relationship. Verse 2 states, "And he became a successful man." Success follows obedience. The Lord was with Joseph because that is how Joseph wanted it. You can have the same thing as Joseph, and success will be your consequence. It is a good consequence to have even though it meant more trouble for Joseph down the road. However, with God, the success always outweighs the failure.

We see in verse 3 that other people are watching us very closely. This is what happened with Joseph, and this is what will happen with us too. People are watching. Here is the dilemma: With success comes great temptation. The higher you go, the harder you will fall. Joseph had much to lose because Joseph had gained so much.

Verse 4 tells us we will find favor with people who do not even know who God is because there are some who notice there is something very special about us. That special something people should notice in our lives is our relationship with God.

I will never forget what Wilmer Brown, an older minister now in heaven whose advice I sought 26 years ago when I was a much younger pastor, told me. He looked at me with sternness in his face and said with deep conviction, "High places are slippery places." Wilmer was giving me a shot over the bow. He was warning me that as wonderful as it was to be working at the church I was assigned to, I was likely to face great temptation. I have never forgotten that. These are all elements that go into combating temptation.

We need to have an awareness of all that goes into temptation. Verses 5 and 6 tell us further of the success and the responsibility Joseph was given by Potiphar.

The last line of verse 6 is important because it tells of the double-edged sword Joseph lived with: He was young, well-built and handsome.

(I have only had one of those three things going for me—and now I am no longer young. I always wished I were built in such a way as to attract girls. There was only one girl that ever saw anything in me and we have been married 30 years.)

It was a blessing to have Joseph's physical qualities, and it was a curse because it elevated temptation in his life. So whatever gifts God has given you, be thankful and at the same time be careful.

Verse 7 nails down the temptation. Joseph was tempted with sexual immorality, adultery. Given how many people mess up in this area, and given the times I've heard the stories in my office, and given the times the subject has crossed my mind, this is a really big deal. This one has swallowed many people who were on the straight and narrow. I urge you not to mess around.

You can forget everything Joseph says in verses 8 and 9 except the last phrase of verse 9. It says, "So how could I do such a great evil and sin against God?" This is what kept Joseph from letting temptation win this battle. Joseph understood that adultery was and is a great evil.

In our culture we have made adultery out to be not that bad. That is part of our problem. We've convinced ourselves there are worse things in life. There may be worse things in life, but that does not change the fact that adultery is a great evil. Recognize it for what it is and you will not be as attracted to it.

Then Joseph makes an important theological statement that includes God, who is in on the dirty little affair being thrown Joseph's way. Joseph recognizes that his temptation, if acted upon, would be sin against God. He was very mindful of what temptation is when it is in full bloom—a huge way to ruin a great relationship with God. When we get this through our thick skulls, we will be a little slower on the trigger with temptation. It helps me to know that it will make a mess of things with God, so I stay further away from the temptation. I think you'll discover the same thing Joseph and I did!

Verse 10 reveals the mind-set of temptation which is "day after day." Do you ever feel like the enemy is never going to leave you alone? Welcome to Joseph's world. You rarely have time to prepare for temptation when it arrives. You prepare for temptation long before it is even a thought.

If I am a teenager and alone with a girl and there is nobody watching and there is presumably nobody who will find out what we are doing, what I do with temptation needs to be decided long before I am in that situation. Have a conversation with others about how to prepare for a storm before there are ever clouds in the sky.

Verse 11 is important to latch onto because it reveals something about temptation, which is "one day." That is how it is for all of us. Have you ever noticed how you can do really well for a long time and then out of the blue temptation comes and we mess up? That is how temptation works. It is a very patient beast. It will wait until you think you are above certain temptations; then it will strike like a coiled snake ready to sink its venom into your bloodstream.

Verse 13 is the best advice ever given in the Bible about temptation. When you're in a tricky situation, sometimes the best thing to do is run.

One summer when I was a counselor at a high school camp, I was in my tent sleeping until I was wakened by a girl sitting on my cot. She asked if I wanted to sleep with her teddy bear that she had brought and she would join us! Yikes! I woke up, sat up, threw her off my bed and ran as fast as I could to the leader's lodge and shared my experience.

It was a close call, but it really wasn't a close call. I had decided years ago that if put in that situation, I would run from the temptation. Little did I know that I would one day face that situation and would have to literally run away from the temptation. Sometimes that is the only solution. If I would have given it some thought, it might have been an entirely different outcome.

It's better to be falsely accused than to be accused and have it be true, right? Joseph was falsely accused and it cost him dearly. His immediate future was awful. But when you honor God even in awful situations, God will take care of you. I would rather be in an awful situation because I honored God than be in bed with Potiphar's wife and hurt my relationship with God. I hope you agree.

Have a conversation with others to discuss why so many see adultery as not that big a deal. Talk about ways to make it a big deal again so we can start dealing temptation some knock-out blows.

The verses that follow tell us that Joseph was punished for a crime he didn't commit. Sometimes life is not fair, but God is always in control even when it looks like He is on vacation. So in verses 21 and 22 we see that even in jail God worked out an incredible plan and Joseph is right in the center of God's plans because of how he handled temptation. I urge you to handle temptation in such a way that God will keep you in His cast of characters who will fulfill His will on this earth.

Joseph is a great example for us because nothing has changed since he lived on earth—at least in this area of temptation. Joseph had lots of things going against him throughout his life. He had siblings who hated him so much they lied, left him for dead, and sold him into slavery. That's dysfunction and victimization all rolled into one family; yet Joseph remained true to God. Joseph loved God far more than the temptation he faced in Potiphar's house. Talk among yourselves and figure out ways you can actually love God more than strong temptations like an affair.

JOB – JOB 1:1–22

The second person I want us to consider is Job. Job is famous for his boils and the suffering he endured. The first chapter in Job presents probably the godliest example of what a human can be in the Bible—and maybe anywhere in the world. So let's learn from the life of Job and see if we can apply a fraction of his character to our lives. Job chapter 1 reads:

> 1 There was a man in the country of Uz named Job. He was a
> man of perfect integrity, who feared God and turned away from
> evil. 2 He had seven sons and three daughters. 3 His estate
> included 7,000 sheep, 3,000 camels, 500 yoke of oxen, 500
> female donkeys, and a very large number of servants. Job was
> the greatest man among all the people of the east.
> 4 His sons used to have banquets, each at his house in turn.
> They would send an invitation to their three sisters to eat
> and drink with them. 5 Whenever a round of banqueting
> was over, Job would send [for his children] and purify them,
> rising early in the morning to offer burnt offerings for all of
> them. For Job thought: Perhaps my children have sinned,
> having cursed God in their hearts. This was Job's regular
> practice.
> 6 One day the sons of God came to present themselves before
> the LORD, and Satan also came with them. 7 The LORD asked
> Satan, "Where have you come from?"
> "From roaming through the earth," Satan answered Him,
> "and walking around on it."
> 8 Then the LORD said to Satan, "Have you considered My

servant Job? No one else on earth is like him, a man of
perfect integrity, who fears God and turns away from evil."
9 Satan answered the LORD, "Does Job fear God for nothing?
10 Haven't You placed a hedge around him, his household,
and everything he owns? You have blessed the work of his
hands, and his possessions are spread out in the land. 11 But
stretch out Your hand and strike everything he owns, and
he will surely curse You to Your face."
12 "Very well," the LORD told Satan, "everything he owns is
in your power. However, you must not lay a hand on Job
[himself]." So Satan went out from the LORD's presence.
13 One day when Job's sons and daughters were eating and
drinking wine in their oldest brother's house, 14 a messenger
came to Job and reported: "While the oxen were plowing
and the donkeys grazing nearby, 15 the Sabeans swooped
down and took them away. They struck down the servants
with the sword, and I alone have escaped to tell you!"
16 He was still speaking when another [messenger] came and
reported: "A lightning storm struck from heaven. It burned
up the sheep and the servants, and devoured them, and I
alone have escaped to tell you!"
17 That messenger was still speaking when [yet] another
came and reported: "The Chaldeans formed three bands,
made a raid on the camels, and took them away. They struck
down the servants with the sword, and I alone have escaped
to tell you!"
18 He was still speaking when another [messenger] came
and reported: "Your sons and daughters were eating and
drinking wine in their oldest brother's house. 19 Suddenly
a powerful wind swept in from the desert and struck the
four corners of the house. It collapsed on the young
people so that they died, and I alone have escaped to tell
you!"
20 Then Job stood up, tore his robe and shaved his head. He

fell to the ground and worshiped, [21] saying:
...Naked I came from my mother's womb,
...and naked I will leave this life.
...The LORD gives, and the LORD takes away.
...Praise the name of the LORD.
[22] Throughout all this Job did not sin or blame God for anything.

There are some amazing passages of Scripture in the Bible like the birth of Jesus, the Cross, the Resurrection and Pentecost, and the Creation account, but apart from those this chapter has to be the most amazing chapter in the entire Bible.

I have gone through the horrors of losing my 16-year-old son. My response was light years from Job's response. So I want very much to learn from this man. I trust as you see him in light of our subject of temptation, you'll gain the deepest respect for Job and learn from him as I have.

There are some chapters in the Bible that are amazing like Job 1. And there are also some verses that are amazing verses like Job1:1. How in the world do you top what it says in verse 1, "a man of perfect integrity"? There is a part of me that says that may be good for him, but that's not possible for me.

Sometimes when I see the mark set so high I want to run from it, but that's not what God wants us to do. God wants us to run to Him. This will produce perfect integrity—or at least it will get us closer to it! Not only was Job a man of perfect integrity, he also feared God. That is what is says in verse 1. The word "fear" is not strictly in the sense of being afraid of God; it's more a matter of standing in awe of Him.

Job had a reverence and a respect and in some regards a literal fear of God. These attitudes toward God help us run away from temptation a little faster. It keeps us from taking God for granted and always applying cheap grace. Verse 1 also states, "And turned away from evil." I suppose if you are a man of perfect integrity and you fear God, the result is going to be turning away from evil.

We always talk about things going from bad to worse. In the case of Job it was a time when things went from good to better! That ought to be our goal too! In your conversations with others, try to figure out ways to accomplish this relationship with God. I'll give you a clue: It begins and ends with relationship. There is not a formula or a trick. It is birthed out of love and grows into a deeper love with God as time goes by. While the Scripture doesn't say it directly, Job loved God more than he loved his wealth and more than his family. Job loved God!

Verses 2 and 3 tell us Job was great among his people because of his wealth. In God's eyes Job was great because of his love for God. In fact in verses 4 and 5 we see that Job's love for God covered his children as well. He feared regularly that they might be doing something against God, so Job made sacrifices to God on their behalf because he valued purity. Job 1:5 says, "And purify them." Purity mattered to Job. Purity should matter to us too.

In your conversation with other people, figure out what God means by purity. Get this one right and you're on your way to knocking the wind out of temptation. The threat of Hurricane Temptation will be downgraded on account of your integrity and your purity.

One other note about Job: Verse 5 says, "This was Job's regular practice." Purity is not a faucet we turn on and off. It is not a switch in the room whereby one minute we choose light and the next we choose darkness. Purity is a river that is meant to flow from the wellspring of our heart. I urge you to tap into this spring and not only define purity but own it. It will cost you less than what temptation is costing you.

The dialogue between God and Satan in verses 6–12 have to be among the most fascinating verses in the entire Bible. When we understand the relationship between Satan and God, we can better understand our relationship to both of them, which has a direct impact on how we handle temptation.

Please note some of the things these verses say. When God asks Satan where he had come from, God didn't say that because He didn't know where Satan was. An all-knowing God always knows! He asked it for our sake.

The Bible was not written because God needs reminders. The Bible was written because we need the reminders. We need the relationship. We are the ones broken—not God! God didn't go anywhere; we did. God never ran away; we did. God does not have a problem with temptation; we do!

Satan answered God's question in verse 7, "From roaming through the earth." If that doesn't scare the wad out of you, I don't know what will. Satan does not sleep. When you are asleep he is awake. Have you ever noticed that porn shops are open 24 hours a day? Satan never sleeps. Satan is standing on your street, climbing over your fence into your yard, looking in your child's bedroom window. Get the picture!

But then God says something that is more amazing than what Satan said in verse 7. God says in verse 8, "Have you considered my servant Job?" This tells us a ton about temptation. Temptation comes only by way of permission from God. This means, as nasty as temptation is, it only comes when God gives Satan permission to use it on us!

Right now, while you're reading this page, Satan is perhaps standing before God saying, "I have taken a stroll around planet earth today." God will reply by saying, "Have you considered my servant ______________?"—and it will be your name. God won't offer your name if you're not ready for the challenge. Remember this about temptation: Every time you get one, it is because God knows you're ready to face that temptation and tell it where to go!

Then in verse 9 Satan says something very interesting back to God: "Does Job fear God for nothing?" Great question, isn't it? In other words, are we fair-weather Christians? Job sure wasn't. It turned out Job weathered the mother of all storms. Are you ready for a storm today?

I love verse 12 because God sets the rules. He tells Satan what he can and cannot do. This is very important when we think about the events of life and evil in the world and temptation. Satan is only allowed to do what God permits him to do.

I know the question on your mind may be, "Why does God permit evil things to happen?" Randy Alcorn answers that at length in his book

If God Is Good. The bottom line is that God is sovereign, which means God is in control. This is a good thing because God does not make mistakes—ever. Whatever He does, it is by design. I don't understand God all the time, but I love Him and trust Him all of the time. When it comes to tragedies in life, you really have one of two options: One, hang onto God for dear life until you get through the rapids of the river, or two, curse God and die. I don't like the second choice very well, so I choose to take the first.

So in the following verses (13–19) Satan goes for broke. FYI, he always does! He destroys all of Job's wealth and kills his ten children. As stated earlier in this book, I have two children, and in 2003 my 16 year-old-son Kevin went home to be with the Lord. I honestly do not know how Job did it. I come up so much shorter than him that I can't begin to express to you how inadequate I feel compared to Job. Yet, I want the strength he had.

So instead of saying I can't attain to Job's stature, my attitude is that I want to have all I can get of what he had in God. That ought to be your attitude as well. Otherwise you have conceded to temptation, and that will only benefit Satan. Imagine you lose your wealth all in one day. That has happened lots of times and people have bounced back. But to lose all your children, whether it be two or ten, is beyond my imagination. But what happens next is even more amazing in the following 3 verses.

In verse 20 it says Job "worshipped." Are you kidding me? My son died and I cried for months. I didn't have an ounce of worship in me. This guy Job was an amazing man. In case you think he must not have loved his children very much to have that sort of an attitude, remember what he did for them as his regular practice in verses 4 and 5. Job loved his children just like any normal parent would.

Job knew something we must not know very well. He didn't have the advantage of Christian television! He didn't have a local bookstore where he could buy the latest Christian literature. He didn't have a seminary or Bible college available to him. He didn't have anything we have today, yet his response was 1,000 times greater than how we respond to tragedy today. We also learn something about worship. It's not about us; it's about God!

In verse 21 Job makes the statement, "Praise the name of the LORD." Are you kidding me? I didn't have an ounce of praise in me for months after losing my son. This guy Job was made of steel.

We learn something else about Job in this chapter. We learn he understands the meaning of the word praise. Praise is not for what we have or have lost. According to Job, praise is defined by who God is. God had not changed for Job. He was still the same. Job remembered something we forget in an entitlement sort of culture: that is that it all belongs to God and whatever we have is not ours but on loan from God!

Then in verse 22 we get the true grit of Job. It says in verse 22, "Throughout all this Job did not sin or blame God for anything." Wow! Job is my hero. I want to learn everything I can from this man of God. Job ought to be who we talk about in our conversation.

We talk about the latest book out or the hottest church in town, or the latest fad in church that is bringing them in by the thousands. Friends, we are missing the mark by a mile. In your conversations, I am inviting you to talk about Job. He is a man worth talking about. A few pages into this story we learn what Job's ultimate temptation is "to curse God and die." Not once in Job's pain and suffering (and there was more that happened to Job after chapter 1) did he change his response of praise to God. If I were you, I'd talk more about Job and less about some of the people we idolize in our Christian culture today. Find me a man greater than Job, and you can make him your topic of discussion. Until further notice, Job is a man worth having a conversation about!

JESUS – MATTHEW 4:1-11

Where do you begin when you're talking about Jesus? Jesus Christ is the Son of God, the King of Kings and the Lord of Lords. Yet, in Matthew 4 we see something in Jesus that we, too, can pull off with Him living in us through the power of the Holy Spirit. This is a classic passage on temptation. There is much we can learn and apply in our lives from this text. I invite you to a third conversation with others from this chapter using Jesus as our third example of how to handle temptation. Matthew 4:1–11 reads:

> 1 Then Jesus was led up by the Spirit into the wilderness to be
> tempted by the Devil. 2 After He had fasted 40 days and 40
> nights, He was hungry. 3 Then the tempter approached Him
> and said, "If You are the Son of God, tell these stones to
> become bread."
> 4 But He answered, "It is written: Man must not live on bread
> alone but on every word that comes from the mouth of God."
> 5 Then the Devil took Him to the holy city, had Him stand
> on the pinnacle of the temple, 6 and said to Him, "If You are
> the Son of God, throw Yourself down. For it is written: He
> will give His angels orders concerning you and, they will
> support you with their hands so that you will not strike your
> foot against a stone."
> 7 Jesus told him, "It is also written: Do not test the Lord your
> God."
> 8 Again, the Devil took Him to a very high mountain and
> showed Him all the kingdoms of the world and their
> splendor. 9 And he said to Him, "I will give You all these
> things if You will fall down and worship me."
> 10 Then Jesus told him, "Go away, Satan! For it is written:
> Worship the Lord your God, and serve only Him."
> 11 Then the Devil left Him, and immediately angels came
> and began to serve Him.

If this passage doesn't get your juices flowing, nothing will. Let's break it down and figure out what we can glean from Jesus.

I have just discussed two great men from the Bible who are worthy of your conversation. However, Jesus has no comparison. He has no equal. Some write Him off because He is God and His temptations were not plausible. Sure they were. But is there a difference between Jesus and Joseph and Job? Of course there is! What I want you to capture from the three temptations Jesus faced is the technique He used. It was a technique we can learn from.

In each of the three temptations Satan used to tempt Jesus, there are two basic points to be made. The first is that Satan used Scripture. The second point is that Jesus used more Scripture!

Satan knows the Bible and church history better than you do. He knows God better than you do! Jesus, when He was at His weakest moment physically, drew on Scripture to combat temptation. If you, my friend, are not spending the time necessary in Scripture to combat Satan and his temptations, then this is where the conversation needs to go.

Discuss with others how life can change in such a way that together we spend more time in the Bible. It will have a direct impact on how we handle temptation. If we fail to avail ourselves of Scripture, then temptation will avail itself on us in a way that will make us all cry!

SCRIPTURES ON TEMPTATION

1. And do not bring us into temptation, but deliver us from the evil one. [For yours is the kingdom and the power and the glory forever. Amen (Matthew 6:13).
2. Stay awake and pray, so that you won't enter into temptation. The spirit is willing, but the flesh is weak (Matthew 26:41).
3. And the seeds on the rock are those who, when they hear, welcome the word with joy. Having no root, these believe for a while and depart in a time of testing (Luke 8:13).
4. Do no deprive one another—except when you agree, for a time, to devote yourselves to prayer. Then come together again; otherwise, Satan may tempt you because of your lack of self-control (1 Corinthians 7:5).
5. No temptation has overtaken you except what is common to humanity. God is faithful and He will not allow you to be tempted beyond what you are able, but with the temptation He

will also provide a way of escape, so that you are able to bear it (1 Corinthians 10:13).

6. But those who want to be rich fall into temptation, a trap, and many foolish and harmful desires, which plunge people into ruin and destruction (1 Timothy 6:9).
7. Therefore, as the Holy Spirit says: "Today if you hear His voice, do not harden your hearts as in the rebellion, on the day of testing in the desert" (Hebrews 3:7–8).
8. No one undergoing a trial should say, "I am being tempted by God." For God is not tempted by evil, and He Himself doesn't tempt anyone. But each person is tempted when he is drawn away and enticed by his own evil desires (James 1:13–14).
9. Then the Lord knows how to rescue the godly from trials and to keep the unrighteous under punishment until the day of judgment, especially those who follow the polluting desires of the flesh and despise authority (2 Peter 2:9–10).
10. Because you have kept My command to endure, I will also keep you from the hour of testing that is going to come over the whole world to test those who live on the earth (Revelation 3:10).

LESSON #8

1. Genesis 3:1–13. Why did God let the serpent mess up humanity?
2. Genesis 39:1–23. How did Joseph beat temptation?
3. Job 1:1–22. How did Job beat temptation?
4. Matthew 4:1–11. How did Jesus beat temptation?
5. 1 John 2:1–6. How can we beat temptation?
6. Forecasting temptation using 1 Corinthians 10:1–13:
   a. What can we learn from people older than us?
   b. What can we learn from church history?
   c. What can we learn from our peers?

7. Helps…
    a. What do you need from the Holy Spirit to help you forecast temptation in your life?
    b. Regarding temptation, are you in need of a miracle from Jesus today? (Perhaps deliverance from an addiction?)
    c. Would memorizing Scripture be of help to you to in your battle against temptation?
    d. Find three of the oldest Christians you know and ask them how they faced temptation and won!

CONCLUSION

Tasing Temptation

We've come to the end of our journey together, but your conversations and your journey are just beginning. What you do with this material could have a great impact not only on your eternity but that of others as well. Christianity has done a poor job in my adult life when it comes to addressing the tough issues. I got tired of not having anything to use as ammunition against temptation. I trust you have gained insight through this book so that you can fight the good fight.

Of course, the bottom line is to follow Jesus. If nothing else, we see how He handles temptation and overcomes it. And that brings us to these final pages.

I have stated in several places that I am a volunteer chaplain for the police department. I see lots of stuff the average citizen doesn't see as I ride around in a patrol car in the middle of the night. There is a whole lot of temptation out there tripping people up like you can't believe.

Thank God for cops! You can't believe how incredible they really are. It is an honor to be associated with them. When considering this book, I thought about what might be the best way to handle temptation. I tried to think of lots of different images. The one that kept coming to my mind was something that I had never experienced before writing this book. I had heard lots of stories about tasing and seen several videos, but I had never personally experienced it myself.

I asked one of my cop friends if it we could set up a time when he could tase me. I wanted to know firsthand how effective it really is. I figured tasing would be a great image for what I'm trying to accomplish with temptation. When I asked my friend, he began laughing and commented he had been dreaming about this opportunity for a long time. I am not sure I wanted to go there, but he said he would take care of it.

Well, the day came for my tasing. Request denied! The captain of the department said that it was not proper training; therefore, it was not permissible for me to be tased.

Not to worry. The department signed me up for EVOC. This stands for wild and crazy driving in a police car without getting a ticket!

I sat in the training room with real cops. I hoped they couldn't tell I was only a chaplain. My instructor singled me out and told me it was time to "rock 'n' roll." We got into the patrol car and I had the time of my life. I learned things I never knew were possible in a vehicle. I was privileged for the next few hours to practice just like the cops, do maneuvers that happen when driving in situations that are dangerous and unique to law enforcement.

It was a rush. I got better as the night went on. I learned techniques I'd never heard of before. As a civilian, I will be a better driver because of this training. EVOC, or Emergency Vehicle Operations Course as it is known to the public, taught me a lot of things about life.

Before sharing the lessons I learned, I have a confession to make. Part way through the training, I got car sick because of the maneuvers we were making and I had to take a break and ultimately went home dizzy. I laid on the couch, went to sleep, and woke up the next morning in my bed with a hangover fit for a fraternity.

I learned that night while in training that the drills I participated in were not practical in my everyday life. I learned that those drills were unique to law enforcement in situations I will never personally find myself in. I learned that those skills were not going to help me on the drive to the store when I need a gallon of milk.

A lot of sermons are like the instruction I received during my EVOC training. While fun and interesting and amazing, the shoe did not fit my foot. What I'm trying to say is that sometimes we ministers are guilty of asking people to do and be what isn't possible. And if it were possible, the road map we draw is hard to read.

The bottom line on temptation is there are no special tricks or training that will give you an edge over the rest of the field. There is no special course that will help you get into the car to get a gallon of milk at the store. Rather, when you go to the counter to pay for the milk and the dirty magazine sits behind the clerk, you will just have to apply truth to help you cope with the temptation.

There is not a magic pill, a magic potion, or any fancy training that will give you protection from temptation.

Ordinary people have to face temptation head-on with no extra help but what has been suggested in this book or any other of a hundred sources. There is no shock treatment out there to help us with temptation. There are no evasive moves we can make with cop cars to get around temptation. Temptation is a beast that demands a face-to-face battle. I believe that if we forecast temptation, we can face down the beast and win the battles in our lives. We can keep ourselves out of the gale-force storms heading our way. It won't be easy. There are no tricks. It is going to take our very best effort. But with God we can forecast temptation and win. With the Holy Spirit we can face temptation and win.

We can keep ourselves out of the gale force storms heading our way. It won't be easy. But with God, we can forecast temptation and win.

I close this book with a passage of Scripture that means a great deal to me. After my son went to heaven I began going through his things in his room. One item, Kevin's Bible, I prize to this day. I had hoped that when I opened it there would be clues to his Christian life. Most boys do not mark their Bibles up a lot. This was the case for Kevin, too.

However, he left just enough for me to be blessed beyond measure. One of the passages he marked up and wrote along the margins is 1 John 2:1–6. It reads:

> 1 My little children, I am writing you these things so that you
> may not sin. But if anyone does sin, we have an advocate with

> the Father—Jesus Christ the righteous One. 2 He Himself is
> the propitiation for our sins, and not only for ours, but also
> for those of the whole world.
> 3 This is how we are sure that we have come to know Him: by
> keeping His commands. 4 The one who says, "I have come to
> know Him," without keeping His commands, is a liar, and the
> truth is not in him. 5 But whoever keeps His word, truly in
> him the love of God is perfected. This is how we know we are
> in Him: 6 the one who says he remains in Him should walk
> just as He walked.

Kevin wrote on the side of his margin in the middle of this section, "Do more than believe, show it by your actions." Christianity is not only about a set of beliefs. Christianity is about our actions that include what we do with temptation too. Let's do the right thing. Let's have a conversation that leads to right actions!

As you seek to forecast temptation and overcome the storms, I pray that God will bless you richly.

APPENDIX

SURVEYING TEMPTATION

This appendix offers a tool for your use—a survey you can use to get a handle on your own temptations—as well as the results of a survey I gave to Christians from many age groups. While I could have asked many more questions, simplicity is best. When I preach, my wife always tells me the shorter I preach the better she likes the sermon!

I pastor a church that has 1,400–1,500 in attendance each Sunday morning. In addition, there are Sunday evening events as well as Wednesday night events for the entire church family. We have a lot of other events during the week for lots of different groups that meet lots of different needs. I distributed this survey to the adults on a Sunday morning and to a college Bible study I teach on Tuesday nights. In addition, both of our youth pastors surveyed their respective groups—middle school and high school. Their results are included as well.

There are eleven distinct ages represented in this survey. The survey itself makes other simple distinctions that will help you know more about how I am able to forecast temptation. You'll be able to do the same if you care to use this with a group you're part of. You have my permission to use this and copy this survey for mass distribution.

My goal was to compile at least 500 survey responses. I received a total of 512. I didn't ask for names since that was not important to this simple piece of research. I learned far more than just stuff pertaining to temptation. I learned important facts about how my church family lives spiritually. If you're a church leader, I highly encourage you to use this survey to learn vital truths about your congregation. If you're a youth pastor, it will give you great insight into the group you are leading. I received far more from this little survey than what I anticipated. Following are a blank survey form for your own use, and the results I received from this survey.

Temptation Survey

Thanks for taking a few brief minutes to fill in this survey on temptation. Please do not give your name. This survey will remain anonymous.

1. Age
   Middle school____
   Senior high ____
   18–25____
   26–30____
   31–40____
   41–50____
   51–60____
   61–70____
   71–80____
   81–90____
   91–100____

2. Please place a number beside each instance, rating it as a source that enhances the temptation to occur (1 is least and 5 is greatest). Temptation to commit a sin comes in the following ways in my life:
   ____When I am tired (1–5)
   ____When I am with a friend (1–5)
   ____When I am with a group (1–5)
   ____When I have not been reading my Bible (1–5)
   ____When I am alone (1–5)
   ____When I am bored (1–5)

3. My most frequent temptation is: (please identify with no more than a short phrase or word)____

____.

4. I read my Bible: (please answer according to your normal pattern and check only one).

____Once a week
____Twice a week
____Three times a week
____Four times a week
____Five times a week
____Six times a week
____Seven times a week
____Less than once a week
____More than seven times a week

5. Do technology and/or media outlets (TV, Internet, Facebook, movies, literature, etc.) contribute to your temptations?

____Yes
____No

6. Please rate your relationship with God by circling only one number. (1 = very poor; 10 = excellent)

1 2 3 4 5 6 7 8 9 10

7. Did you grow up in the church?

____Yes
____No

8. How long have you been a Christian?

____Less than 1 year
____1–5 years
____6–10 years
____More than 10 years
____More than 25 years
____More than 50 years

Thanks for taking time to fill in this survey. It is being used for research and as a model survey on temptation, to better help church leaders address this universal issue.

THE RESULTS

I conducted this survey during a Sunday morning church service. It became an interactive tool so that my congregation knew I wanted to communicate with them on a universal subject that in the church is mostly avoided.

We speak in general terms, but rarely are we specific when it comes to the subject of temptation. I expressed to the congregation that this provided an opportunity for me to feel the heartbeat of the culture within the church. I presented it as a tool so we could interact with one another, promising to share the results with them as I preached. This is one way to accomplish the goal of being a better listener to where people are in their spiritual journey.

The following is a breakdown by age of the results of the survey. It was extremely helpful to me. I trust it will be insightful for you as well, both as you see yourself in it and as you see more clearly the struggles others face.

There were 512 who took the survey at Salem Evangelical Church. The breakdown in age is as follows:

Middle school – 65
Senior high – 60
18–25 year olds – 49
26–30 year olds – 27
31–40 year olds – 35
41–50 year olds – 67
51–60 year old – 92
61–70 year olds – 69
71–80 year olds – 40
81–90 year olds – 6
91–100 year olds – 2

I will give the summary totals after first breaking the survey down by age groups. Both ways of analyzing this material may be helpful for you to read and digest. It was extremely revealing for me to learn the following data. While the age demographics may be different, based on being churched or unchurched I think we will discover some very obvious trends that can help us better deal with temptation.

MIDDLE SCHOOL

There were 65 surveys turned in by middle schoolers (sixth to eighth graders). On the second question I counted only responses that received a 4 or a 5 in the survey. The results are:

Tired – 7
Friend – 11
Group – 8
Not reading Bible – 15
Being alone – 15
Boredom – 13

Interestingly, in this age group, on the second question, the top two vote-getters were *not reading their Bible* and *being alone* as being the times when temptation is the strongest.

Their response to the third question is as follows: There were 21 different answers with only four items receiving four votes or more. They were: *lying*, *video games*, *stealing*, and *television*. It's important to note that in the mind of a middle schooler these may not be related to sin as much as simply to the temptation of what they do with their time. This will become much more evident as I share the results from the other age groups.

The fourth question has to do with the amount of time spent reading the Bible each day. The average number of days a week a middle school spends reading the Bible is 2.77. There were 20 who read it only one time a week, while there were three who read it more than seven times a week. There were nine who responded that they didn't read it at all.

The fifth question dealt with the correlation between technology and temptation. I thought the response would be higher; I was wrong. There were 41 who said technology played a part in temptation while there were 24 who said technology had nothing to do with the temptations they face.

I love asking the sixth question. It is of course a subjective question relative to what people think "good" is. The cumulative average answered by this age group was 6.95. In all, they think they are doing fairly well as Christians. They are probably right!

The seventh question told me a great deal about the dynamics of our church family. Forty-five of the kids who responded to the survey said they grew up in the church, while there were 16 who did not grow up in the church. This becomes even more revealing as the ages go up, as you will see in the following pages.

The eighth question is a little tricky with this age group because of their young age compared with the other age groups surveyed. Nonetheless, their response is important. Fifty-one of the middle schoolers surveyed had been Christians for more than six years. It means we're doing a great job of reaching our children at a young age in our children's ministries while at the same time we are weak in reaching the unchurched!

Senior High

Concerning question two, which needed to receive a 4 or higher to be registered, the results were as follows:

Tired – 3
Friend – 16
Group – 19
Not reading Bible – 22
Being alone – 17
Boredom – 8

The response of the senior-high group compared to the middle schoolers in this category is very different. We see in the high school years what we have always known—that friends have an impact on decisions this age group makes. It reminds us of the impact friends have on how we behave.

The third question brought with it 18 different responses. But from these 18 responses, there were two that stood out above the rest by far and away. The number one response was *purity*. The number two response was *cussing*. There were no other answers even close to these two responses. This gives me clear direction with this age group. Again, I don't believe this information is new, but it is current in that some things never change. The difference is I am not guessing.

The fourth question deals with frequency in reading the Bible during the week. The senior high group spends 3.2 days a week in the Bible. This is higher than the middle schoolers. (As the age of the groups increase, you'll notice that time spent in the Bible trends upward.) The sad part of this question is that I learned there were 15 who spent no time in the Word at all! This is alarming, but not surprising.

On the technology question, there were 40 who said technology plays a part in their struggle with temptation while there were 19 who said technology has nothing to do with their temptation. Again, this is not how I thought the survey would trend. I thought it would trend much higher toward technology.

The high schoolers collectively saw themselves come in at 6.40 in how they thought they were doing as Christians. Again, this is purely subjective, yet important. I'm pleased that it was as high as it was. It shows they are living in the right direction with room for growth.

Of the 58 who responded to this question, there were 53 who grew up in the church, leaving only five who have not. (Two who took the survey did not answer this question.) This tells a great deal about the culture of our church. It tells me where we have come from and, if no changes are made, where we are going. It tells me strongly that while we're ministering well to those within the church, we're doing a less than adequate job of reaching those outside the church.

It would stand to reason that how long a person has been going to church would match the previous question to some degree. Fifty-one of the students who responded have been going to church for six years or more with a whopping 31 who have been going to church ten years or longer. Again, this was a survey on temptation. My surprise was to find out far more than stuff on temptation. I learned a great deal about the people I go to church with and the people we are reaching and the people we are not reaching.

18–25

I thought seriously about combining this age group with the next age group. Yet, I discovered their answers were just different enough that it was wise to keep them separated. I understand the trend to reach the 18–35 year olds, yet I would argue from this survey that their needs are quite different from one end of the age group to the other. I hope this is helpful for those ministering to these age groups.

I currently minister to 18–30-year-olds in a Bible study on Tuesday nights at our church. This survey was helpful for me because I learned they are not all on the same page as is sometimes assumed.

In response to the question on when temptation comes, their responses were as follows:

Tired – 7
Friend – 5
Group – 4
Not reading Bible – 24
Being alone – 18
Boredom – 7

This question was very revealing. This age group associates most of their struggle with temptation with *not reading their Bible*. A strong second-place finish was when they were *alone*. This is what I expected; yet when you see it on paper it hurts because these are real people with real struggles.

The third question, which dealt with one's most frequent temptation, the one that came away with the most votes by far was *lust*. *Sex* came in a distant second. There were 13 responses in all. Unlike the middle schoolers and senior highers, the responses of this age group are much more serious offenses.

The cumulative time this age group spent in the Bible each week was 3.39 days. Sadly there were 11 who said they do not read their Bible at all. By this point in life, if patterns of Bible reading are not being established, then it usually takes a major event in life to bring someone around to spending more time in the Bible and thus with God.

The fifth question again came out a bit surprising to me in that 39 out of the 49 said technology plays a role in temptation while ten said it had no role at all. I thought this would be higher, but I was wrong. So, we can conclude that at least 20% of the time technology is not to blame for temptation. There are other things out there in the world that don't require electricity that are just as electrifying!

I was pleased to see this age group gave themselves a rating of 6.51 as a Christian. It's a good sign to see this group leave themselves room for growth, yet not rate themselves so low that they allow stuff into their lives that will take them away from God.

As with the other two age groups, the seventh question is definitely trending toward being churched. This age group responded with a 43–6 margin of those who grew up in the church. And along with that it is not a surprise that 35 of the respondents have been Christians for more than ten years. The first good sign I saw on this question was there were seven who have been Christians for five years or less! It's a good sign for me because it means this age group is reaching out to people who are not as churched.

26–30

There were 27 who responded from this age group. About the second question their answers were as follows on the subject of sources that enhance temptation:

Tired – 5
Friend – 3
Group – 2
Not reading Bible – 14
Being alone – 10
Boredom – 5

This is much like the previous group. We can note that the older a person gets, the less they are influenced by their friends. This is not new news, but it is good to be reminded what makes each age group tick.

This age group was all over the board on their most frequent temptation, so I will list all of them for you:

Food – 5
Lust – 2
Anger – 3
Thoughts – 1
Alcohol – 2
Swearing – 1
Shopping – 1
Gossip – 2
Sexual – 5
Lying – 1

I don't even know what to make of this broad range of answers except to report them to you and let you decide what it means.

The results on the fourth question for this age group place their cumulative answer at 3.93 days a week that they read the Bible. This age group is spending more time in the Bible than the ones just younger than them. I found this to be interesting. There were also only three who didn't read the Bible at all! This is a good sign and a good trend!

For the first time with an age group, their answer to the technology question was about what I would have guessed it would be. There were 21 who said technology plays a role in their temptations. There were only six who said technology had nothing to do with temptation in their lives.

When they rated how they were doing with God, they received the highest self-grade of all the age groups thus far with a cumulative 7.04. This is a really good grade given the age group. I'm going to give them credit for wanting to be close to God and they see it that way too!

Not surprisingly, given the previous answer and the other answers from this age group, 25 out of the 27 grew up in the church. The correlation from answer to answer with this answer is quite high.

On the last question about how long they have been a Christian, the answers were not surprising either, which is good when you're looking for trends and answers to behavior issues. Sixteen have been Christians for more than ten years while eight have been Christians for more than 25 years. Again, this is a very churched audience that answered this survey.

31–40

There were 35 people in this age group who answered the survey. There were three responses that stood out to me in response to the second question, regarding where they experienced enhanced temptation. Those three in order were: *not reading the Bible*, *being alone*, and *being tired*. This makes sense and follows a pattern that was being established if you go back and read what I've previously reported on the younger age groups. We begin to see the place fatigue plays in temptation as one gets older.

The answers to the third question about the most frequent temptation surprised me, in that I didn't see a pattern but rather another across-the-board response to temptation in general. Their answers were as follows:

Pornography – 5
Anger – 4
Lust – 3
Food – 4
Sex – 3
Gossip – 2
Swearing – 2
Alcohol – 3
Materialism – 1
Television – 1

What do you notice in the results? I notice that Satan uses anything and everything to trip people up.

On the fourth question dealing with time spent in the Bible, this group gave themselves a 3.00. If we compare this to the other age groups, we see something new in the results. This is the first age group where there were a large number who were in the average range of this group. The extremes were smaller and the middle ground was greater. This is a good sign as far as I'm concerned.

On the question of technology, we see a leveling off of the impact of technology by this age. There were 19 who said technology played a role in their temptation, while there were 16 who said technology had nothing to do with their temptation.

On question number six where they rated how they were doing as Christians, they gave themselves a cumulative 6.94. This number is fairly consistent with the other groups.

On question number seven about growing up in the church, this age group is a bit different from the other age groups in that 23 grew up in the church and only 12 didn't. This is important because this is the first age group in my survey to have so many who didn't grow up in the church.

On the question pertaining to how long they had been Christians, there were 19 who had been Christians for more than 25 years while there were ten who had been Christians for more than ten years. There was only one who had been a Christian for less than a year, two who had been Christians for 1–5 years, and only three who had been Christians for 6–10 years.

41–50

There were 67 people who responded from this age group. In this group and the next several, I got a really good sampling of where people are living in relation to culture. They also are the parents of many of the younger people I've already reported in this survey. It would be very interesting to note the connection between parents' behavior and how their children behave.

On the second question the results are as follows:

Tired – 12
Friend – 6
Group – 5
Not reading Bible – 27
Being alone – 27
Boredom – 15

This group showed some very strong feelings about not reading their Bible and being alone and being bored and being tired. They are the first group to have four areas so close to one another in number. This is worth noting.

On the question of the most frequent temptation, there were 16 answers that were given. I found it interesting that there were two that stood above the rest and one of those stood above its nearest competitor. *Lust* was number one by a landslide, and *anger* came in a distant second. As we have learned from other studies, there is a connection between lust, pornography and anger. This study will not analyze that point other than to note the point.

The cumulative answer given to question number 4 on time spent in the Bible each week is consistent with the other age groups. This group gave themselves a cumulative 3.74. I really don't have a comment one way or the other on this point. I would note, however, that this number reflects spending more than one-half of the week in the Bible!

The impact of technology on temptation recorded by this group is very similar to what the previous group gave as their response. There were 36 who said technology played a role in their temptation and there were 31 who said technology had nothing to do with temptation they face.

This age group gave themselves a cumulative score of 7.23. This is by far the highest of any of the age groups to this point. They see themselves as doing pretty good as Christians. Temptation is just a part of being a Christian is how I read their score.

This question of growing up in the church is an interesting one for this age group. Their answer was different than all the other age groups: It was evenly split for this age group with 33 who grew up in the church and 33 who didn't. However, whatever time they spent away from church must not have lasted long because there were 38 who said they had been Christians for more than 25 years, while there were 20 who had been Christians for more than ten years. There were six who had only been Christians for 1–5 years and one who had been a Christian for less than a year. This was encouraging to me because this age group has some new blood in it!

51–60

This age group was the most interesting to me because it is my age group (granted, I'm on the younger end of it!), so I was very interested in what others my age had to say about temptation. There were 92 who responded to this survey from this age group. This is the highest number of participants of any age group surveyed. I'll comment more about this when a give general summary statements after reporting the stats from each individual age group.

Like the last group there were four responses to question number 2, which lists the scenarios that most frequently enhance temptation. Coming in first, with 43 responses was *not reading the Bible*. Coming in second, with 27 was *being alone*. Coming in third, with 19 was *being tired*, and coming in fourth, with 18 was *being bored*. These are the same four that were mentioned by the previous age group. This is a definite trend to track when dealing with temptation. By using the results of this survey, we can identify four clear areas that need to be addressed when forecasting temptation.

The most frequent temptation is going to blow you away. I am going to list the number one answer last. There were 15 responses in all including: Internet, spending, smoking, worldliness, worry, lying, swearing, gossip, alcohol, lust, sex, television, and anger. Guess which single category got the number one answer? *Food!* I'm not going to say another word—yet.

This age group spends more time in the Bible than the previous age groups. Their cumulative answer was 4.21 days a week. Very interesting is the fact there were 13 who spend more than 7 times a week in the Bible. This was an encouraging sign to see. There were only eight (though far too many) who spend no time in the Bible at all!

On the technology question, it was evenly split again except for one. There were 42 who said technology played a role in temptation while 41 said technology had nothing to do with their temptations. Given their answers to the second question, I do question the accuracy of their responses to this question. I think there is more of a connection than what the survey is reporting!

They rate their Christianity at 7.12, just about what I would expect given the answers from the other age groups.

This age group reported 63 who grew up in the church and 26 who didn't. For the first time in reporting age-level responses, this age group (because they are old enough) had 16 who had been Christians 50 years or longer while there were a whopping 55 who had been Christians for 25 years or longer. There were but two who had been Christians for less than one year.

61–70

Sixty-nine people responded from this age group. They were consistent with the previous age group in that, in order, the top four things that made them feel more vulnerable to temptation were: *not reading the Bible*, *being alone*, *being tired*, and *boredom*. However, not reading the Bible was by far the top vote getter.

This age group listed 20 strongest areas of temptation. Coming in first, with seven votes, was *food*. Coming in second with seven votes was *sex*, and coming in third with six votes was *anger*. I suppose what surprised me most was not that food was at the top but that sex and anger were numbers two and three. I will say more about this in the general summary at the end of the chapter.

This age group spends a lot time reading the Bible. Their cumulative score was 4.64 days a week. That is very good given their age and their busy lifestyles. There were only four out of 67 who don't read their Bible at all. While four is too many, I'm glad the number isn't higher.

This is the first age group since the youngest ages where technology plays less of a role in giving in to temptation. There were 28 who said technology plays a role in their temptation. There were 40 who said technology had nothing to do with their temptation. This would be what I'd expect from this age group.

This age group rates their walk with God higher than all the others with a 7.72. This is a very high score. If there ever were an age when people would score themselves close to God, it should start happening with this age group. Well done!

This age group had 45 who grew up in the church while there were 24 who didn't. Likewise, there were 29 who had been Christians for more than 50 years while there were 35 who had been Christians for more than 25 years. All the other responses combined were only five. This age group has spent a long time in church and a long time being Christians!

71–80

There were 40 who responded from this age group. We are blessed with lots of older wiser Christians in our church. They did not mark very many spaces that contributed to temptation. But of the ones they did mark, they listed *being alone*, *not reading their Bible*, and *being tired* as the top three vote getters.

There were 16 most frequent temptations, with nothing really jumping out at me. Only *food* received four responses, with each of the others receiving three or less. Nothing new came to the surface from items previously listed with other ages, except for one that noted *griping*. It seems that food is a factor with all the ages and the older one gets the greater the temptation of food becomes. I will say more about food in the summary portion of this chapter.

This age group spends 5.53 days a week reading their Bibles. It appears the other ages can learn from this group in that by this time in life, Bible reading moves to the top of the priority list. For the first time in the age groups, this age group has everyone reading their Bible at least one time a week. There was not a single person who didn't read their Bible at all in this age group. Praise the Lord!

Surprisingly, on the technology question, there were 17 who said technology played a role in their temptation. My hunch is that represents a lot of television watching. Obviously, it would include the food channel! There were 22 who said technology had nothing to do with their temptation of choice.

This age group gave themselves a rating of 7.98 as Christians. Would you agree with me there is probably too much humility in this age group? They should probably give themselves a 10! However, they can teach us that no matter how old we are, there's always room for growth in the Lord!

There were 27 who grew up in the church and there were 13 who didn't. Nobody who responded had been a Christian for fewer than 10 years. There were 28 who said they had been a Christian for more than 50 years!

81–90

There were so few who responded in this age group that to trend anything is difficult to do, yet I thought you might find their responses interesting. There were six who responded from this age group.

Two of them said *food* was a temptation while one still deals with *anger*.

They gave themselves a 5.17 times a week in the Bible, and I believe that may have to do with their health. I don't think it is a spiritual issue like it is with the other age groups.

One said technology plays a role in their temptation while four said technology played no role at all.

They graded themselves at 8.17 in how they were doing as Christians. Like the last group, I think they were being a bit too humble!

Four of them grew up in the church, one didn't, and one didn't answer. All six have been Christians for at least 50 years!

91–100

Yes, in my church I was blessed enough on the day of the survey to have two people in this age group who filled out the survey. Neither indicated much on what aided temptation. However, you'll love their most frequent temptation. One person listed *playing bingo*, while the other did not like it when someone talked about them. Even though we might smile at their "issues," these were very real to them.

Together they read their Bibles six times a week. They were probably old-school enough not to count Sunday.

They rated their Christianity a *ten*. I would hope when we are all that close to heaven that it had better be a 10 too! Both had grown up in the church and both had been Christians for longer than 50 years.

While some of these individual age groups are of interest to you and me, the summary of all of them is most fascinating when taken as a whole.

Summary

At the beginning of this chapter I gave you a breakdown of the number of participants from each age group. Now I'm going to give you the rest of their cumulative story. Please keep in mind there were a total of 512 who responded to the survey. It is possible on question number two to have more than 512 total answers while with the other questions there will likely be less than 512 because not everyone answered every question.

The things that most contributed to temptation in order of frequency are as follows:

Not reading the Bible – 198
Being alone – 149
Boredom – 84
Being tired – 77
Influence of a group – 52
Influence of a friend – 50

When taken as a whole you can get a great picture of how to forecast temptation with greater certainty and effectiveness.

The third question was about listing the most frequent temptation. Taken in order of frequency and taking all 512 responses, their combined answers are as follows:

Lust, pornography, Internet, sex, television – 134 (Instead of giving you the breakdown for each of these five items, I consider them to be under the general category of sexual purity.)

Food – 57
Anger – 30
Cursing – 19
Alcohol – 16
Lying – 12

There are many things about this list that catch my eye. First, I am not surprised that the category of *lust* and its cousins are number one. I'm shocked that *food* is number two. This caught me totally off guard. Yet, in my own life, I will admit, I struggle with food addiction!

I'm shocked that *anger* is number three, although others have said they aren't surprised with this one at all. I expected something lower on the list to be in the third spot. So, in my opinion, based on this survey there are three major areas I need to focus on when addressing the subject of forecasting temptation: purity, food, and anger!

Question number four about how much time is spent in the Word is not relevant as a whole, given the way I have broken it down in age groups. Yet, the fifth question, when combining the answers, does tell me something important: 57% of those surveyed say that technology has a hand in temptation, while for 43% of the respondents it does not. I need to address how we can better use technology for good and not harm.

Likewise, question number six stands best when broken down by age groups and not compiled as a whole.

However, on question number seven I learned that 72% of those attending Salem Evangelical Church on that day grew up in the church while 28% did not grow up in the church.

On the final question, I learned that 93% of the people who took the survey have been Christians for six years or longer. And I learned that when you take out the younger age groups, that percentage is even more skewed. My conclusions outside of the survey are that I am not reaching enough people who are not saved!

People are coming to Christ all the time at our church. However, this simple little survey has shown me much more than what I bargained for. It is a tool that will guide my future life and my future ministry. I trust you can use it for your situation as I have mine. Imagine what the responses would be if the demographics were younger and even less-churched! That may well be your situation. Either way, the truths taught in this book will help you, whatever your demographics may be.

Acknowledgements

I am grateful to the good people at Deep River Books for seeing the potential in this project. They have been professional, encouraging, and good friends to me. I especially want to thank Rhonda Funk, Kit Tosello, and Bill and Nancy Carmichael.

The cover design is by Jeff Miller, a professional graphic design artist. He is far more than that to me. I met Jeff as a young boy when his family became part of our church family. The Millers have been good friends over the many years we have been together. I watched Jeff grow through the years and watched his talents blossom. It has been a joy to partner with Jeff on this project.

I am a pastor—not a writer, per se. So I am grateful to my editors, Sue Miholer and Rachel Starr Thomson, who made this project much cleaner and brighter than what I first submitted. I am convinced editors are the unsung heroes behind every good book.

I dedicated this book to law enforcement and particularly to the agency I have been assigned to: Keizer Police Department. For seven years, I have thoroughly enjoyed being their chaplain. They are some of the most amazing people you will ever meet. Their ability to act and react with virtually no notice is amazing to witness. Their skills far outweigh their pay. To every law enforcement agency that serves and protects the communities of this great country—we owe them our gratitude. What I appreciate most about the Keizer Police Department is their genuine friendship!

I have a great friend who is a pastor in the same denomination I serve in. We have been friends since shortly after graduating from the same college. Jon Strutz is one I have worked with, played with, laughed with, and cried with. We visit often throughout the week. I highly value his friendship.

I am grateful to God for my family. I thank God for my wife Joanie. I thank God for my daughter Kristi. I thank God for my son Kevin. I am a blessed man!

Another Powerful Resource from Dr. Randy R. Butler

He won't be texting you or sending you an email, and you won't find Him on Facebook. So where *is* God when you need Him the most? Randy Butler asked himself that very question after the sudden death of his sixteen-year-old son. Once Randy finally became silent, God answered all the questions in the pages of his soul, and Randy found God Himself.

Reclaiming Heaven's Covenant, God's Blueprint to Restore All Relationships teaches you to connect with God and others in way that will affect your marriage, how you raise your children, your job, finances, and more. Develop healthy, long-lasting, and loving interpersonal relationships that connect heaven with earth.

"In *Reclaiming Heaven's Covenant*, Randy opens God's Word and lets us in on his life journey. He is honest, wise, and true to Scripture. He emphasizes genuine relationship, and doesn't reduce the Christian life to principles. Rather, he focuses on knowing God personally and walking with Jesus. I'm a better person for knowing Randy Butler and I think you will be too."

—Randy Alcorn
best-selling author of over thirty-five books, including
Heaven; *If God is Good, Why do We Hurt?* and *Courageous*

CONTACT THE AUTHOR:
Randy@RandyButlerBooks.com
www.RandyButlerBooks.com

For media and booking inquiries,
please contact Rhonda Funk at Bring it On! Communications
Rhonda@BringItOnCommunications.com